A FUNNY THING HAPPENED ON THE WAY TO THE BEACH*

*When an Extraordinary God
Reveals Himself to Ordinary People*

By CHRIS MARSHALL

Exulon
ELITE

A Funny Thing Happened On The Way To The Beach*
*When an Extraordinary God Reveals Himself to Ordinary People
by Chris Marshall

Printed in the United States of America.

Edited by Xulon Press.

ISBN 9781498483506

www.xulonpress.com

Table Of Contents

Dedication ix
Endorsements xi
Acknowledgements xv
Introduction: A Funny Thing Happened on the
Way to the Beach! xvii

Chapter 1 A Funny Thing Happened at the Doctor's Office 25
       Coincidence?
       Like Father, Like Son?
       Sinner, Sinner, No Chicken Dinner
       Unexpected Grace
       I'm Going to Be a Pirate!

Chapter 2 A Funny Thing Happened in Sunday School 38
       You're Going to Be a Preacher
       An Electrifying Moment
       America's Got Talent, but Mine's Not Baseball
       A New Direction … I'll Show You!
       God Is Still Working!
       God Got in the Way
       Finding Miss Right
       No, Sir

Chapter 3 A Funny Thing Happened in a Nursing Home 58
       What to Do?
       Family Reunion
       Who Are My Friends?

You're a Failure
Here's to You Mrs. Robinson
A Good Idea — Not God's Idea
One More Person at a Time
Don't Pursue a Career in Public Speaking
Paying the Bills
Miss Right to Mrs. Marshall

Chapter 4 A Funny Thing Happens in Marriage. 78
Honey, I'm Going to Be a Pastor
Choosing a Seminary
God at Work
Only Greek Makes Sense to Me
A Pastor, Mentor, and Friend
When ENFP Lives with ISTJ
The Memorable Dr. Willis
There's Nothing of Interest
Why Did I Wear My Pirates' Sweater?
I Need a Computer

Chapter 5 A Funny Thing Happened at the Hospital. 101
The Move
Baptism by Fire
I Don't Want to Work
Pack Your Bags
Can You Come?
No Problem
Time for Children
Hopeful Grief
Out of the Mouths of Babes
It Is Time for You to Leave
Why Does Everybody Want Me?
The Big Vote

Chapter 6 A Funny Thing Happened in the Kitchen 124
The Big Vote (Continued)
When God's Timing Inhales
A Vision of the Church

You Can't Always Have Your Dreams
Once a Youth Pastor
Leftovers
Challenging the Status Quo
Experiencing God
A Vision of the Lost
No Need to Pray
Do You Know What You Need?
A Vision of the Tombstone
The Explosion
Speak to Me God!
Breakthrough
The Second Explosion
When Push Comes to Shove
Finished and Free

Chapter 7 A Funny Thing Happened in a Storm Door 156
The Amazing Beginning
If God Wants Us to Go
Let's Move
The Big Mistake
Always Darkest
Land, Ho!
A Strategy at Last
Information – Application = Information, but...
Send Us Men
The Tragedy That Brought Triumph
It Doesn't Matter What You Believe
Half Measures
When Everything Is Going Right and Nothing Is
The Next Right Thing
Ordinary People
Extraordinary God
The Solution

Dedication

To Nancy, my wife, who has shown me how our extraordinary God works in and through ordinary people; more than anyone I have ever known.

Endorsements

The Rev. Dr. Chris Marshall mentored me in the gospels; is the longest standing board member of the ministry I serve; and is a real friend. I've witnessed the Lord's hand in his life closely for the past ten years. I remember hearing about every jump shot Abby took in high school. When people tell me they'd love to go do Missions but they can't come up with $2,000, I tell them about a pre-teen girl named Emmy Marshall who collected aluminum cans from her neighbors each year to pay her own way. And in all this Nancy stood, with God's strength and perfect poise, ready to serve all with exactly what they needed. Pastor Chris painted my bedroom when my wife Jess and I had returned from the mission field and were expecting our first child. While painting, I took a call from the pastor of a megachurch that supported us. After the call, Pastor Chris said, "Maybe when I'm the pastor of a megachurch, I won't have time to paint your bedroom." Now God is creating His megachurch through New Life. Why? Because Pastor Chris, though extraordinary to all of us, carries a very real understanding that his God is the One who has given him every gift he has. If any of us called him with a real need, he'd be there to serve it. Enjoy this book and know its principles have influenced thousands to be extraordinary.

—Pastor Matthew Geppert
President South East Asia Prayer Center www.seapc.org

The Bible says God planned each day of our life before our first day came to be! But if you are like me, you have added some experiences through your humanness. Chris's book will help you experience God who promised to work for good in all things, as we love Him and obey His voice. Life can be funny, challenging, and crazy sometimes. Thank you Chris for helping us to experience God's goodness at all times!

—Pastor Jim Graff
Senior Pastor Faith Family Church, Victoria, Texas

Is there anything more terrifying than a five-year-old with a shotgun? Connecting the dots in his grace-filled life, Chris Marshall tells that story and many others with great tenderness and beauty, illustrating the unrelenting chase of God in his life. What a story! I loved this book and I know you will too.

—John Hall
Producer and Co-Host: *The Drive Home with John and Kathy*
101.5 WORD-FM, Pittsburgh, PA

All of us need to know God is present in our journey. Chris takes the mask off of everyday Christianity and reveals the faithfulness of God in one man's journey to follow a Savior. You will be encouraged to abandon yourself to Jesus. I don't want to spoil it for you, but wait until you read about the time he tried to murder his mother. Seriously, this book is the real thing. Get ready to be inspired to believe God for great things in and through your life. Chris and I have been friends for many years and I have witnessed his steps of faith personally. I have watched him and Nancy journey into the unknown and obey Jesus when it cost them everything. He is a man after God's heart and is sold out to the kingdom of God and his family. I count it an honor to call him my friend.

—Pastor John Nuzzo
Senior Pastor Victory Family Church, Cranberry Township, PA

As I read *A Funny Thing Happened on the Way to the Beach,* * it became apparent God's thread of grace was strategically woven through each of Chris Marshall's stories, which are deeply rooted in his faith and trust in Jesus. I am proud to call Chris a great friend and mentor. I had the opportunity to work with Chris directly on Glade Run's Building Team. He helped us hear God's call to increase the youth program, incorporate a Christian preschool within the church's ministry, add a gym, expand the fellowship hall and upgrade the kitchen so we could accommodate a Meals-on-Wheels ministry. His vision, revealed by our extraordinary God, led to that upgraded facility becoming a conduit for an increasing number of people coming to know Jesus. All of the "funny things that happened along the way" to Chris reveal how we, as ordinary people, live within God's grace. We see how God speaks to each of us through His written word, invites us to participate with Him through prayer, calls us to action through our particular circumstances, and gives us guidance and direction though other believers.

— Ken Rieger

Vice-President and Co-Founder, *G & R Investment Consultants, Inc.*

In *A Funny Thing Happened on the Way to the Beach,* * Chris Marshall unabashedly shares his personal journey of faith and frustration; of tragedy and triumph; and how his walk with God has molded him into the man he is today. We expect to learn about an individual account of God's relationship with man. What we discover is one man's journey is really every man's journey; that God is with us every step of the way if only we take the time to notice Him. And that *ordinary* is all a matter of perspective. Chris skillfully uses the art of storytelling to convey an engaging, thought-provoking, and potentially life-changing message everyone needs to hear.

— Dr. Joseph Tsai, D.C.

Founder of Back to Life Chiropractic, Gibsonia, Pennsylvania

Acknowledgements

Every book is the result of countless lives impacting one—the author's. I am grateful to God for speaking into my life every day through His written word, prayer, life's circumstances, and the people He has sent my way.

I want to thank Nancy, for letting God use you to speak into my life for more than four decades. Your words and life have shown me Jesus in more ways than I can list. I appreciate your love for Jesus, me, our children, the people of the churches we have served, and so many others we have met in our journey together. Most of all I thank you for staying with me through everything, especially in those times when God's voice was clear to me, but not so clear to you in that specific moment.

A special thanks to our daughter Emmy and my brother Kenn for lending your editing skills and encouragement. Emmy, thanks for challenging me to press into the theme of the book—hearing God's voice in my life—as well as for your suggestions for making it more accessible to a broader audience. Thanks too, for the great revised chapter titles.

Kenn, thanks for your journalistic expertise and facility with English grammar. Your attention to detail has ensured a much "tighter" read for all who pick up *A Funny Thing Happened on the Way to the Beach.** I do think you may have enjoyed correcting my mistakes a little more than necessary.

Thanks to both of you for giving me a most precious gift—the gift of your time and talent—in reviewing and revising my content.

Thanks to Ron Kirin for pushing me to consider who and why, and for being bold enough to help make sure I knew. Thanks too, for suggesting a far better title than my original.

Thanks to Brian and Tammy Summers for their faithfulness in and through tragedy; for reviewing *A Funny Thing Happened* for factual content; and to Tammy for finding several word redundancies and omissions the rest of us had missed.

Thanks to so many of you whom God has used to speak into my life at particular moments, when I so desperately needed to hear from Him. Whether I mentioned you by name in *A Funny Thing Happened on the Way to the Beach** or not, my life has been enriched by yours.

Thanks to all of you who have chosen to read *A Funny Thing Happened on the Way to the Beach.** I pray God speaks to you through it and that your lives are encouraged, challenged, and transformed.

Introduction:
A Funny Thing Happened
on the Way to the Beach!

Have you ever taken the time to stop and reflect on your life? Do you do it regularly? In May of 2015, I decided to take a week away to do some planning and to write my third book. Since life had been moving fast, and mostly in desired directions, the timing seemed right for a retreat. While driving to South Carolina, I thought about how long it had been since I'd taken a week away to be alone, to step back, and to regroup. The answer shocked me — never.

I've been part of many retreats, conferences, mission trips, and family vacations over the years, but I had never invested an entire week by myself to rest, reflect and focus on a particular task. I already had the outline for the book — *Real Men*. The content would come from a course I'd taught for a men's group at New Life, the church I serve as lead pastor. Since my first two books had taken only a few days to write after outlining them, I assumed the retreat would be a great way to knock out another.

It didn't work out that way.

I was staying at Myrtle Beach in a condo about a half-mile from the ocean, and decided to take a walk the first morning to invest some time in prayer. As I walked through a couple of dunes and caught a glimpse of the water, I headed south. Although it was overcast, walking on the sand, watching the immensity of the ocean stretching out to the east, and hearing the crashing waves, gave me a deep sense of God's majesty and presence. Random thoughts poured through my head as I tried to pray. Eventually, I asked, "God, what do you want from me?" Life had been going so fast. I sensed it was time to get back to basics.

Instantly, I heard, "I want to be with you." The clarity of the message caught me by surprise. Be *with* me? God is with me all the time. Reflecting on the words, I realized while my days had been filled with times of prayer as I thanked God for what He had done, or asked Him for advice to meet a challenge, or petitioned Him to meet my needs, I wouldn't say I sensed God was with me.

I thought of the gospels, which tell us the night before Jesus called the twelve disciples He would apprentice to carry the Good News to the world, He prayed all night long. Then He called those He wanted to be "…with Him." (See Mark 3:14.) They were also called to preach, heal and cast out demons, but the first call on their lives was to be with Him.

Many times over the years I've been reminded God calls us human *beings,* not human doings, because who we *are* is far more important to Him than what we do. Only once we know who we are — and particularly who we are in Him — can we do what He calls us to do. God wanted to be with me. The God of the universe wanted to be with *me*! I smiled. Then I laughed. This was going to be a great week.

I had left my phone at the condo on purpose, so it would be only God and me. I didn't know anyone there, so I wouldn't be interrupted. I walked for an hour before turning around, which gave me two uninterrupted hours with God. As I walked and watched the beauty around me, I thanked God, and listened for anything else He might have to say.

Eventually my thoughts turned to the book I was planning to write. As I thought about it, I started thinking about Leda Gromley, my maternal grandmother. I hadn't thought about Grandma Leda in a long time. Something she said to me when I was a teenager came to mind, "Chris, you need to plan your life as if you're going to live forever, but live your life as if Jesus were coming back today." At first it seemed like a random memory. What did that have to do with living as a real man in today's world? The more I rolled the thought around in my mind, the more it seemed God must have brought it there for a reason.

Suddenly it hit me—this had happened many times over the years. Sermon and book ideas have come to me in the very same way. All of the books—now numbering a couple dozen—remained in the idea or outline stages, except for two. The idea for another book crystalized. I already knew its title: *Life Planning: Because You're Probably Going to Live Longer than You Think.*

In an instant, I started debating with myself. I had already started writing *Real Men.* What point could there be in developing yet another book outline? Nevertheless, as I rolled it around in my head, the details became vivid. I couldn't wait to get back to the condo and start typing. As soon as I got back and sat down, the words flowed. The outline came together more easily than any I've ever written. I moved on to the book's introduction and then the first chapter.

The book outlined a process for planning one's life based on developing major life goals first. That incorporated Grandma Leda's idea about planning my life as if I were going to live forever. If I were actually going to live forever, then I'd want to accomplish many important goals. After that it was simply working backward to a particular week — the current one — and creating a plan to live in the moment in such a way as to fulfill each of the significant goals over time. That would help me maximize the present by recognizing how much I needed to accomplish, because Jesus might come back at any moment.

As I invested time on the book that week, and over the next several months, I realized something — the process seemed great and seemed likely to work, but I wasn't using it myself. How could I write a book about something I wasn't doing in my own life? The litmus test of *Life Planning* must surely be it had turned my life into a well-disciplined example of the principles it espoused.

My initial excitement for the book had come from the reality that I needed its truths and the systems it proposed more than anyone. I've always been able to see the big picture, and to set huge goals. I've even been able to challenge and convince others to join me in pursuing them, but getting to the planning and execution of the details necessary to accomplish the goals has never been my forte.

As I reflected on the dilemma of writing a book to help folks do a better job of planning their lives, while not using its principles myself, I realized something else: My first two books had virtually written themselves after I outlined them because I was so passionate about their subjects. I've always dreamed of being a well-disciplined, well-organized person and leader, but as someone said, "A dream without execution is a hallucination." *Life Planning* was still a hallucination for me. Until I moved it into the realm of reality, and put the processes to work in my own life, *Life Planning* had to go back on the "Books to Write" list.

Maybe you've been there. You've had a great idea—and it *was* a great idea—but as you sought to put it to work in your own life, it didn't work for you. Maybe it will become a truly great idea for your life down the road, but right now it's nothing more than a good thought. We all need good thoughts to store in our minds, and thoughts for the future when we're ready for them. We also need to live right now.

When I realized I'd invested six months working—or more accurately—*not* working on my latest book, I was discouraged. Then I remembered my "Books to Write" list. As I reviewed it, the list contained a couple of dozen book ideas that do excite me. Several folks had been asking me to write one of them recently. They wanted me to write a book detailing God's interaction with me over the years. Specifically, they wanted to know how God had spoken to me in particular situations.

As I thought about that particular book idea, I remembered what had excited me about the incident on the beach, when I changed the focus of my writing from *Real Men* to *Life Planning: Because You'll Probably Live Longer than You Think*. It presented another example of the extraordinary God of the universe choosing to interact with me, an ordinary human being. God wanted to be with me—again! He has done that over and over throughout my life.

That's what God does. He wants to be with you and me, not because we're notable or famous, not because He wants to make us notable or famous, but because He loves us—each one of us, as if there were only one of us. How incredible. When we know that and believe it, we change. The change starts on the inside, but eventually becomes apparent to others.

People around us sense the difference. It causes conflict or brings resolution, depending on whether people grasp the reality that there is a God who cares about human beings, and not human beings in general, but each of us human beings in specific or denies that truth. Over the years, many who have heard me talk about God's dealings with me—His personal dealings with me—have asked me to describe what it's like.

This book is about one human being, named Chris Marshall, with whom God has wanted to spend time, but it's so much more than that. It's a call for you to see through common everyday moments that God invites you to be with Him too. As we look at "snapshots" from my life, you may be reminded of moments in yours when God has revealed Himself to you. Through those snapshots we'll see God is real and that He believes in us.

The reason I titled the book *A Funny Thing Happened on the Way to the Beach*(*Or What Happens When an Extraordinary God Reveals Himself to an Ordinary Person)* is because of all the different ways God has shown Himself to me; the ways He has invited me to be *with* Him; the times and the situations when He has revealed Himself. Some of those moments didn't seem like times when God would reveal Himself. Those were "funny" things, in the sense of strange or odd. At other times, God has shown up in the middle of "funny," meaning humorous situations. Sometimes it was "funny," because no one could've seen it coming. The precipitating event for writing this book ultimately was that moment on the beach when God told me He wanted to be with me, and my attention was drawn to Grandma Leda's quote. The funny thing is, I'm writing a book that has little to do with Grandma's quote, but everything to do with God's interaction in an ordinary person's life.

While many folks don't even believe God exists, and others see God either as a vague, nebulous force, or a vindictive, cosmic judge, the pictures of God you'll see here, and the many ways He has interacted with me through the years, may challenge or comfort you depending on your view of God. At times you may think, *That's not God!* Other times you may think, *God is too serious for that.*

When Jesus walked the earth as God in the flesh, many people said He wasn't serious enough. Others said He was a blasphemer, because He saw Himself as God. In the end, the "church" people of the day turned Jesus over to the Romans to be executed. He hadn't fulfilled their picture of what God ought to be like. If there were ever a "funny" thing, in the sense of odd or strange, it was the God of the universe chose to humble Himself and come to earth as one of us for our benefit.

Whether you're a Christian or not, whether you believe in God or not, my hope is you will find *A Funny Thing Happened on the Way to the Beach** entertaining. I hope you will see glimpses of God that you may never have imagined. Who knows? He may even reveal Himself to you! That's my hope. Thanks for joining me as we journey through one ordinary life and experience some of the funny things that have happened along the way.

Chapter 1

A Funny Thing Happened at the Doctor's Office

Coincidence?

W here do you start when the goal is to help folks see glimpses of an extraordinary God who reveals Himself in an ordinary life, through the funny things that have happened along the way? Where would *you* start? Maybe the best place is at the beginning. For me, the beginning of funny things happening along the way was July 6, 1943. That's the day Tom Marshall, my next older brother, was born. Tom was a big baby. When I say big, I mean huge. He weighed more than eleven pounds. While that surely provided interesting conversations for family and friends when they heard the news, it did much more than that for me. Tom's birth compromised my mother's reproductive system. The doctors told her she would never have another child.

Only she did.

Thirteen years after Tom was born, Mom went for a routine physical exam. The doctor told her medical advancements had made it possible for her to have some surgical repairs, which would enable her to have more children if she wanted. She talked it over with my dad. They decided to talk about the possibility of having more children with my brothers Tom and Jim. Jim, who was fifteen, was all for it. He said he'd love to have another brother or sister. Tom was only half committed—he was interested only in having brothers. Mom and Dad complied. About a year later, on June 7, 1957, I was born—a baby brother for Tom and Jim. Then came Kenn about two years later; a fourth boy for the Marshall family. You may see a handful of funny things in all that, right? Most folks who had been told thirteen years earlier that they would never have another child would have thought two sons were fine. That would've been it. When those sons had moved into their teenage years, if those same parents were told, "Oh, by the way, if you want to have more children *now*, it's possible," most parents would have said, "No, thanks!" Not Clyde and Ruth Marshall. To that I say, "Praise the Lord!" After all, who would have written this book if they had decided two boys were enough? Or if the doctor had never offered Mom the option? Or if Tom hadn't "demanded" they have boys?

Many people believe everything happens by random chance or coincidence—small things such as babies being born under improbable circumstances, and big ones such as the creation of the universe. Others believe something beyond us created everything and guides human life. I belong to the latter group of believers. Too many coincidences occurred in my *even* being here to write this book for me to see them as coincidences. After all, Tom had to be so big when he was born that Mom wouldn't be able to have any more children. A doctor had to tell Mom a surgical fix for her inability to have children was available thirteen years later. Mom and Dad had to decide to have more children, when their two sons were teenagers, and then put it to a family vote. And Tom had to lobby for another boy or boys. All of those things happened, and here I am, and not only me, but Kenn too. That's funny, don't you think?

Like Father, Like Son?

Clyde Marshall, my dad, came from a long line of angry men. When I say angry men, I mean men with bad tempers. When things didn't go their way, they erupted. They yelled. They threw things. If they tried to fix something and it didn't go well, they broke it. Growing up in that environment, I developed a temper of my own. I've never known whether it was nature or nurture or both, but when things didn't go my way I yelled and threw things, too. It started early. I was that way for as long as I can remember. One time when I was five years old, Mom sent me to bed before dinner on a Sunday evening for some infraction of the family rules. (An important detail—Dad worked away from home most of the time. He usually left on Sunday afternoons and then returned either the following Friday evening, or two Fridays later. That meant on the evening in question, my Dad had left for the week shortly before the incident.)

Instead of going to bed as I had been told, I decided to go to my Dad's closet, load his rifle—a Winchester .32 Special—and shoot my mom. Yes, I said *shoot* my mom. That's a drastic action, but it shows the extent of my anger problem, even at the tender age of five.

Being so young, and not knowing much about guns, I loaded the shell in the rifle backwards. I knew enough to realize the shell was backwards. I couldn't remove it, so I put that gun down and picked up Dad's 16-gauge shotgun. I loaded it correctly, pointed it toward the floor in the direction where I thought Mom was on the floor below, cocked the hammer, and pulled the trigger.

That produced a loud bang, a big hole in the closet floor, and a horrified scream from Mom. She ran up the stairs to the bedrooms. Instantly realizing I was in big, big trouble, I descended the stairs at a high rate of speed and ran past Mom and Chuck, a teenage cousin who was visiting. I made it all the way to the basement, and started pushing vigorously against the garage door. It was one of those old-fashioned kinds that was in one piece and pushed out from the bottom. Unfortunately for me, I was too small to push it open.

Mom caught me, picked me up, spanked me, looked into my defiant little eyes and said, "Chris Eugene Marshall, are you ever going to do that again?" (You know it's not funny when Mom uses the middle name.)

Through my tears I shouted, "If I get mad enough I will!"

Wrong answer.

Mom spanked me again. Then she asked, "Are you ever going to do that again?"

Believe it or not, I'm a relatively bright person, so although I was still shouting, *If I get mad enough I will!* in my mind, what I said was, "No."

Mom's next words were the ones I never wanted to hear, but especially not then, since it was early Sunday evening: "Wait until your Father gets home!" I knew what I had experienced from my mom were love pats compared to what was going to happen when Dad came home on Friday. To say I "sweated bullets" all week might be an exaggeration, but apropos given the situation.

Sinner, Sinner, No Chicken Dinner

After my brief exchange with Mom, I had to go to bed without dinner. Once I got there and calmed down a bit, I realized something that has been extremely helpful to me throughout my life: *I am a bad person, a sinner,* I thought. I've attended church most of my life; when I was a little boy, many of the preachers focused heavily on the reality that we're all sinners who need to believe in Jesus, to repent of our sins, and to trust Jesus in order to be saved. After attempting to shoot my mother, I couldn't pretend I was a good little boy, or even a basically good little boy. I knew the preachers were right: I was a sinner. That has helped me every day, because it freed me from fruitless attempts to become a good person through my own efforts. I know I have never been one, am not one now, and will never become one no matter how hard I try. Therefore, a number of years later, I trusted Jesus as my Savior and Lord, knowing any goodness in my life would come from Him and having His Holy Spirit live in me.

Those statements fly in the face of modern and postmodern thinking. Many say good and evil don't exist. We're all random collections of matter, our impulses driven by chemical and electrical impulses and reactions. Others think we're all "basically good." We only need a little tweaking here and there.

I'm thankful I recognized so early in life that I'm not a basically good person, and that no amount of tweaking will fix me. Having lived through nearly six decades on this planet, I'm certain no one else is basically good either, at least none of the ones I've encountered. When the Apostle Paul wrote a letter to a church in a place called Galatia nearly 2,000 years ago, he reminded the people that even after we trust Jesus as Savior and Lord, we each face a lifelong struggle between the Holy Spirit's guidance in our lives and the *flesh*, or the *sinful nature*.

We all endure being creatures with a sinful nature by virtue of being born into a fallen world. The sinful nature doesn't get better. It doesn't grow up and become good. We can't take it to therapy and make it better. (I'm not saying therapy isn't helpful, simply that it doesn't make us good either.)

Once we become Jesus' followers, we receive the Holy Spirit—the Spirit of God within us. Even that doesn't make us good. We must give the Holy Spirit control on an ongoing basis. When we do, His goodness comes out in our lives. When we don't, the inherent evil still comes out.

That doesn't mean we'll be as bad as we could be. It means we'll never be or become good by virtue of our efforts. It's a funny thing that so many people can hold on to the idea or belief that they're basically good, when an honest appraisal of our own actions over the past twenty-four hours would demonstrate the falsity of that. If it's been a particularly good twenty-four hours for you, then turn on the news. You'll probably hear an example of someone whose neighbors, co-workers, or friends are attesting to what a *good* person he was. The reason for their comments is this good person had committed a heinous crime, and they didn't see it coming.

In Jesus' day, the *best* people were the Pharisees. They were members of a strict sect of religious Jews. They believed sincerely they were good people. When Jesus came along, He challenged the Pharisees at every turn. He reminded them that their self-righteousness was not righteousness in the eyes of God, and that simply because we say we're good doesn't make it so.

Jesus offended the sensibilities of the Pharisees. He wasn't impressed with their obedience to the letter of the law, because they often held little concern for its spirit. That was a major area of contention between Jesus and the Pharisees. They were inclined to live out the literal letter of the law, as they interpreted it, while Jesus emphasized the heart or spirit of the law.

The Apostle Paul was a Pharisee before his conversion to faith in Jesus, so he understood better than anyone how much we must rely on the Holy Spirit's power in order to live God's goodness. He had invested the first decades of his life learning and living the Law of Moses to the letter. Once he was transformed by his relationship with God through Jesus Christ, everything changed. He experienced God's grace and power to transform a human being, and he came to understand the ultimate law is God's grace and truth, lived out in love.

I'm grateful for that horrendous moment when I was five years old, and pulled the trigger of my dad's shotgun. That sounds funny, being grateful that I attempted to shoot my own mother, but in that instant, any doubt I might ever have held or would one day develop about the kind of person I was or am melted away.

God didn't speak audibly to me in that moment, but in a real way it was the first time He ever spoke to me. I had not broken the letter of the sixth commandment: you shall not kill, since I didn't kill my Mom, but I had failed to exercise love toward her. God showed me a reality the Bible teaches from start to finish: human beings since Adam and Eve are not basically good. We're sinners.

Some who have heard me tell this story have said, "You were so young. You didn't know any better." The truth is I knew exactly what I was attempting to do. Thankfully, I wasn't big enough at the time to carry the gun downstairs and aim it accurately. For those who have been thinking, "It was your Dad's fault. He ought to have locked the guns in a safe place." No argument there. Even so, it was I, not my Dad, who pulled the trigger. The blame is on me, not him. If I had gone to bed as I was told, the incident would never have happened. Thankfully, it did happen. Otherwise, I might have grown up under the myth of my own goodness. I might never have come to understand my need for God so early in life.

Unexpected Grace

I'm sure Mom told Dad about the incident with the gun during one of their phone conversations that week. She might even have called him that night, given the severity of my offense. Each day that week seemed like two or three to me, as the impending return of Dad on Friday loomed over me like a dark cloud. Finally, Friday came. When Dad walked through the door, I made sure I wasn't there to greet him, as I often was. I was "playing" out back. When he eventually called me inside, I shook with fear. As I walked into the house, Dad sat on the living room sofa holding his Winchester rifle. He looked at me, pointed to the bullet lodged in the gun backwards and said, "Do you see this?"

I nodded my head tentatively.

"Do you realize if that shell had gone off you could have been hurt, even killed?" he asked.

I nodded my head again.

Then Dad said, "I don't ever want you to touch any of my guns again until you're twelve and I can teach you how to use them properly. Do you understand?"

I nodded a third time. That was it. No yelling. No throwing things. No spanking. I received a calm presentation of the truth that I could've been hurt or killed, and that guns were not for me until I was twelve. What was that?

Grace.

Who could have expected that? Dad wasn't a Christian when he spoke those words. I was only five years old. I didn't understand fully what was going on at that moment, but as I've reflected on that meeting with my Dad dozens of times over the years, I've realized he showed me grace. I deserved to be punished. Yes, my Mom had already spanked me—twice—but my Dad was the one who meted out the punishment for serious "crimes" in our family.

All week long, I had expected to be punished. I knew I deserved it. It was right for me to pay the consequences of my actions. I didn't know what Dad would do, but I knew whatever it was, I would remember it for a long time. I was right. I've always remembered it, but not for the reason I had anticipated. It was one of the funniest things that ever happened to me: In an instant Dad extended grace to me. When I think of grace, I think of that moment when Dad held that rifle in front of me and explained clearly and calmly what could've happened, and that I would be permitted to use it when I was older. Dad gave me a pass; I didn't deserve it. That's grace.

You might be thinking, *I never tried to shoot my mom. I'm not that bad.* To be sure, attempting to shoot your mother is extreme, and yet each of us demonstrates our need for grace every time we fall short of God's standard to love one another, and to live in His truth.

You and I deserve to be punished for our sins, for rebelling against God and for putting ourselves on the thrones of our own universe, but Jesus walked calmly to the cross, died in our places, and paid the penalty we deserved. The Apostle Paul described it so well in Ephesians 2:8–9:

> [8]God saved you by his grace when you believed. And you can't take credit for this; it is a gift from God. [9] Salvation is not a reward for the good things we have done, so none of us can boast about it.

What an incredible gift! We deserve to be punished. We receive grace. Jesus, the Son of the living God, died on the cross to pay the penalty we owed for our sins, and to offer us a new life, a life of grace and truth. That life is lived here and now, and it continues into eternity.

I would never have thought I'd learn the reality of God's great grace in Jesus Christ at the age of five by attempting to shoot my Mom, and then having my Dad extend it to me, but I did—my sin, Dad's grace. Eventually it became my sin, God's grace. You might not believe in sin or grace. Those of us who do, understand a funny thing happened on our way to being punished for the sins of our lives: Jesus died to pay the penalty so we may experience His grace and live lives that are radically different from average lives. They're so different because they're based on grace, forgiveness, truth and love. More on that later, but I hope this glimpse of a potentially disastrous moment in my early life has given you the gift of understanding that you're not a good person, either.

Once we understand we're not good, and only then, may we understand God's goodness has given us grace. That grace transforms us here and now and one day will give us eternal life with God forever. Once we've received that gift, the rest of our lives become a grateful response to it. Knowing we're not good, and experiencing God's grace, shows us how extraordinarily good God is.

I'm Going to Be a Pirate!

The final slice of my early life I want to share is my first vocational aspiration. I wanted to be a Pirate—not the kind who sails the seven seas, and steals other people's stuff—I wanted to be a Pittsburgh Pirate. When I was six or seven years old, I decided I wanted to be Willie Stargell's replacement when he retired. I had done the math and determined when I was old enough to be a major league baseball player Willie would be old enough to retire from playing leftfield for the Pirates. This was more than a childhood dream—it was that—but I invested countless hours practicing and playing baseball so I could make it to the big leagues one day. I didn't let the reality of living in Gipsy, Pennsylvania, a tiny town with only about a hundred people and only a handful of boys my own age, keep me from the dream. I dragged Kenn to the baseball diamond day after day when no one else would play. We would go out to the outfield and I would have him throw line drives at the fence, so I could dive and catch them or at least give it my best effort. The point was to get over my fear of running into a fence if I ever needed to in order to catch a fly ball during a game.

Two of our neighbor boys hated baseball, but sometimes agreed to come and play for a while if I agreed to play with their Tonka trucks with them first. I detested playing with Tonka trucks as much as they disliked playing baseball, but it was a worthwhile trade to me because I loved baseball that much.

Over the years, Gipsy had a team for teenagers only once. I was eight years old, but tried out for the team anyway. I made the team, and played center field, not because I was so good, but because we often had only nine players counting me, so I had to play. The pitchers on the opposing teams were typically fourteen or fifteen, so I either struck out or walked nearly every time I batted. I still loved being part of the team, and my dream of playing in the "bigs" kept growing over the years.

What does that have to do with our extraordinary God and His interesting ways of showing up in ordinary people's lives? What does it have to do with how He speaks with us?

To be honest, not a lot, but it was through baseball and other sports that I learned most of the discipline I had in my early life — and discipline is a vital part of living as Jesus' followers. I learned to work hard because I wanted to be the best baseball player I could be. Later, that held true when I played football and basketball as well.

Showing up for practice day after day, especially when playing on teams that weren't very good and the prospects of winning were slim, taught me to persevere. My personality lends itself to spontaneity and doing whatever feels best in the moment. (Thus, attempting to shoot Mom when I was five....)

As I've already mentioned, planning and detail are not my forte, but through sports I learned to delay gratification in order to gain new skills, benefit the team, and accomplish goals. That has served me well in my many decades of serving Jesus through the church and beyond.

It was often frustrating to play on teams when some or many of the other players didn't work hard or give their best; but even that taught me to interact with others in both positive and negative situations. I'm grateful to those who invested in me as coaches, because they instilled in me the desire to help others to learn the skills I have in sports and in life. They showed me how to encourage discouraged teammates and how to challenge ones who weren't giving their best to do more. God has used sports to make me a more effective husband, dad, pastor, mentor, and friend. The funny thing is I thought I was merely getting ready to play left field for the Pittsburgh Pirates.

Chapter 2

A Funny Thing Happened in Sunday School

You're Going to Be a Preacher

Here's a funny thing: about the same time my dream of becoming the left fielder for the Pittsburgh Pirates was taking root and blooming in my mind and heart, a Sunday school teacher took me aside and said, "Chris Marshall, you're going to be a preacher some day."

I thought that was funny, so funny I laughed out loud. I knew it wasn't polite to laugh at adults, especially one who was telling you something she thought was quite serious and special, maybe even a message from God. But I thought she was joking. We'd been through a lesson on Jesus telling His disciples that if they had faith as big as a grain of mustard seed, they could say to a mountain, "Be cast into the sea," and it would "listen."

During our snack break, I slipped outside, went behind the church where there stood a pretty big hill and with all the faith I could muster said, "Move!" Believe it or not, the hill didn't even quiver. I was devastated, because I was sure I had at least as much faith as a grain of mustard seed. Mustard seeds are extremely small. I tried again, "Move!" Nothing. Again, "Move!" Still nothing. After a few more tries, I concluded I had *zero* faith and went back inside to console myself with some Kool-Aid and vanilla wafers. I said to the teacher, "Bernadine, I don't have any faith. I went outside and told that hill to move and it didn't."

That's when she said it. That's when Bernadine said, "You're going to be a preacher some day." I laughed. I thought she was crazy, and wrong, since I had no faith. But the seed was planted, and one day it would sprout.

An Electrifying Moment

One hot spring day a few years later, my Tonka truck neighbors, Bruce and Tom and I were walking on the McMillan hill. As we walked along, a huge bolt of lightning struck a tree a couple of hundred yards away. The noise of the impact caught us by surprise. It had been sunny, but in a moment the sky darkened and a thunderstorm threatened. As we ran home, Bruce said, "If that lightning bolt had hit me, it wouldn't matter, because I got baptized a couple weeks ago so I would've gone straight to Heaven."

I was eleven at the time, but Bruce's statement didn't seem right. The way I'd heard it at church and in my Bible reading was it was Jesus who saves us, not being baptized. A much more intimidating thought struck me: *If that lightning bolt had hit me, I would be in Hell right now because I haven't responded to Jesus' offer of salvation.* I was sure God was offering me the opportunity to receive His salvation.

The funny thing is I didn't accept it, not until more than a year later. For some reason, even though we had an "invitation hymn" every Sunday at the end of worship at Gipsy Christian Church, a time when people could go forward to announce their commitment to Jesus, I don't remember anyone ever walking forward at the end of one of those hymns. The only time anyone went forward was at the close of summer vacation Bible school. So, as we ran home that day, I decided I would go forward at the end of vacation Bible school and ask Jesus to be my Savior and Lord.

Bible school came a few weeks later. In those days it lasted for two weeks. About the middle of the second week, a girl said, "I bet you can't jump from that top step (where I was standing at the moment. It was outside the front door of the church entrance) to the bottom!" Of course, I could. After all, gravity was on my side. It was only six or seven steps, and a girl had bet me I couldn't do it, so naturally, I jumped. I made it — gravity being on my side and all — but as I landed my right ankle turned sharply. The force of the landing stretched some ligaments, which was quite painful. If the girl who made the bet hadn't been standing there, I would've cried.

The injury was bad enough that I couldn't walk. Why is that important? Because in a few days I was supposed to walk forward to ask Jesus to be my Savior and Lord as we closed Bible school. What to do? I had crutches, but I wasn't going to walk forward to ask Jesus to be my Savior and Lord while using crutches. I have no idea why I thought that would've mattered to Jesus. One of the ladies in the church offered to carry me forward. Right. How would that look to Jesus? Remember, I was eleven years old, and an extremely independent eleven year-old at that. I decided to wait another year.

That's funny, don't you think? I've often wondered whether I would've gone to Hell in the ensuing year had I died, because I purposefully rejected the opportunity to trust Jesus as my Savior and Lord. I know now that I could've simply trusted Jesus at any moment, but I had it in my mind that I needed to do it "officially" at the close of Bible school.

I wonder how many people wait to trust Jesus until some future moment when the conditions are precisely right. G.K. Chesterton once said most people don't say, "No," to Jesus. They say, "Not yet," and they say it all their lives. We can always find a reason to put off trusting Jesus, and starting to live under His guidance and care. I did trust Jesus the following year, and have often wondered at other times when I've put off responding to His call in various moments of my life, what blessings I've missed along the way because of my delay. Have you ever wondered that?

America's Got Talent, but Mine's Not Baseball

I didn't let Bernadine's idea that I would be a preacher someday, or committing my life to Jesus when I was twelve, get in the way of my dream of playing left field for the Pittsburgh Pirates. I kept practicing all I could in Gipsy. Then when I was fourteen, the opportunity came to play on a "teener" league team in Hillsdale, PA. It was six miles away, but Kenn and I often rode our bikes to practice when Mom couldn't drive us. That's how much we wanted to play baseball.

I did well. I was one of the best players in a league with not that many players, but the success fueled my dream. Eventually, I started playing in a couple of adult leagues when I was seventeen.

At first I didn't get to play much, but eventually I did, and we even had a former minor league player on one of our teams. When given the opportunity, I played well, batted over .300 and thought, "Who knows? Maybe I am going to be the left fielder for the Pirates."

Then one day a friend asked me to play on his team for a weekend tournament in Rossiter, PA. It was close to home, and an opportunity to play more baseball, so I said, "Sure." The opposing team had a major league pitching prospect on the mound that day. He was left-handed, as am I, and he had a legitimate ninety-miles-per-hour fastball; the first — and last — one I would ever have the opportunity to face in a game.

I sat on the bench for most of the game, as I expected, being a last-minute add-on to the roster. I knew my main role would be as a pinch hitter or to fill in late in games. My teammates had fared poorly against the major league quality fastball. Finally, in the last inning I got to pinch hit. I walked to the batter's box confidently, waiting to see what this guy had, sure that whatever it was I would hit it.

The funny thing is I didn't exactly see the first pitch. I saw a blur and heard it hit the catcher's mitt. The umpire yelled, "Strike!" Then came the second pitch — I swung wildly and quite late. Strike two. I thought to myself, *He has me 0 and 2; he'll throw his curve.* He did. It was about eighty-five miles per hour and broke sharply from the outside corner, down and across the plate. Strike three. Take a seat.

In that moment I realized something. God didn't need to tell me audibly or otherwise — *I'm never going to play left field for the Pittsburgh Pirates.* I wasn't quitting or giving up. I continued playing baseball, and later softball, and enjoyed it for many more decades. I was facing reality.

The show *America's Got Talent* features Americans who have various types of talents. The performers we see on the show are the ones with enough talent to move us or entertain us. Many more don't make it to the show. They don't have enough talent. When it came to baseball, I played well enough to be good and to have fun, but not well enough to even consider making baseball a career.

Although my dream of playing major league baseball had developed early, the dream had grown as I moved into my teenage years. Now, I also wanted to be rich and famous. Baseball had seemed even more the way to go, because professional athletes get both fame and fortune, and I loved playing baseball so much. What could be better than getting paid to become famous, for doing something you loved?

Realizing baseball wasn't going to be my ticket to fame and fortune didn't end my dream of pursuing it. It only changed the direction. One of the funny things that happens in America is people say, "You can be anything you want. You can do anything you want. If you work hard enough; if you study long enough; if you discipline yourself enough; you can be and do anything you want."

As a follower of Jesus, I believe the Apostle Paul's words to the Philippian Church, "I can do all things through Christ who gives me strength." I don't believe that means a five-foot-four, 119-pound teenager can one day be the left tackle for the Pittsburgh Steelers; or that someone who can't hit a ninety-miles-per-hour fastball will play in the major leagues—unless he can throw one.

Each of us is given skills, talents, and abilities. Those who know Jesus have spiritual gifts as well; but the truth is few of us can do *anything* we want. The best thing for each of us is to learn who we are and what gifts, skills, talents, and abilities we have. We must develop them, train to use them, and become the best we can at whatever it is God has created, gifted, and skilled us to do for His glory. Whether you believe in God or not, you have skills, talents and abilities. You might attribute them to genetics, chance, or hard work — and all of those play roles in their development. The Bible tells us even the ability to work is a gift from God; that every good and perfect gift — which would certainly include natural skills, talents, and abilities — comes from God.

It's great to dream. I've always had dreams from that first one of playing left field for the Pittsburgh Pirates, to today's dream of sharing, growing and living the new life of Jesus Christ with the world — one person at a time. Those dreams, when sifted through the reality of our spiritual gifts, skills, talents and abilities, and applied with planning and detail can produce amazing results. The results might differ radically from our original dreams, but they'll be amazing results all the same.

At the end of the day, when I say we can't be anything we want, it's not to discourage us. I want to encourage each of us to understand that our unique design suits us ideally for greatness in a particular area — when we find that sweet spot, it makes all the difference. Our lives will be much more meaningful for others, and much more satisfying to us. Do you know your gifts and skills — your sweet spot? Are you using them to pursue your dreams?

A New Direction…I'll Show You!

About the time I realized major league baseball wasn't in my future, a funny thing happened in math class. We had finished for the day and Mr. Sebastian, the teacher, asked us an important question, "What do you think you're going to do after high school?"

Remember this was in the early 1970s, and the school was Purchase Line High School in Commodore, Pennsylvania. Purchase Line was a small, rural school. Many of my classmates, who numbered a little more than a hundred, weren't thinking of college. I was. After all, I was planning to become rich and famous.

Baseball was out, but I had a cousin who was going to the United States Military Academy at West Point. I had thought about going to West Point because a guidance counselor had suggested it might be a good fit for me. When I mentioned that to my parents, their eyes brightened. I had also reasoned to myself that if I went there, I could get a great education, serve my country, then get a law degree and go into politics. Who knew where that would lead? Fame and fortune via door number two. (Any *Let's Make a Deal* fans?) Anyway, when Mr. Sebastian asked me, I said, "I think I'm going to West Point."

He said, "That's a great school, but I don't think you could get in there."

While baseball was no longer in my future, I was an excellent student with better than average athletic ability, two traits that would be valuable at West Point. Having already been a follower of Jesus for several years, I knew the importance of honesty, courage and other character traits that would also serve me well as a cadet. When I heard the statement, "Great school, but I don't think you could get in there," I thought, "I'll show you."

I did.

I took the physical and academic aptitude tests for West Point, and received a recommendation from our local legislator. The offer of an appointment to West Point came the following December. For a moment, it was great. No one could remember anyone from our school having gone to West Point. Now, I would join my cousin, Keith, as the only other family member to go there. Everyone was excited for me. But there was a problem. I knew I wasn't supposed to go there. After all, I had applied in the first place mainly to prove to a teacher that I could get accepted. It would certainly be a viable path to wealth and fame, but something else was now on the table: I had recently experienced a very powerful demonstration of God's work in my life.

God Is Still Working!

That experience started indirectly when Kenn, my younger brother, had the cornea of his eye torn during basketball practice. He was taken to a local hospital, evaluated, and scheduled for surgery the next day. That evening our pastor, Andy Weigand, and I went to visit Kenn. Before we left, Andy said, "Kenn, would you mind if I prayed for God to heal your eye?"

Kenn said, "It couldn't hurt, right?" Andy prayed. We left. The next day, when I came home from basketball practice after school, the plan was to go to the hospital and visit Kenn. (Back in those days hospital stays were substantially longer than they are now.) When I walked into the house, there sat Kenn watching television with no patch on his eye and everything fine. He explained when the doctor had come into the room to check his eye before surgery it was healed. The doctor was amazed. He said it wasn't possible for Kenn's injury to have healed itself over night. Kenn said Andy had done it. The doctor didn't buy that explanation, but there sat Kenn watching television. Kenn has always been quiet and reserved so he took this incredible news quite evenly.

I, on the other hand, did not.

I ran to Andy's house, which was about a quarter of a mile away, jumped up the porch steps and knocked loudly on the front door. When Andy answered, I shouted, "Andy! Andy! Kenn's eye is healed!"

"Praise the Lord!" Andy responded.

I asked, "Andy, what happened?"

"What do you mean, what happened?" he asked.

I said, "How did Kenn's eye get better?"

"We prayed and God answered," he said.

"Andy, that doesn't happen," I said. What I meant was I had never seen it happen, and I didn't think it still happened in our day. I believed the accounts of healings and other miracles from the Bible, but I didn't think they still happened.

Andy said, "Then you explain it." I couldn't.

Andy took me through a number of biblical passages from the Book of Acts that spoke about the Holy Spirit coming to believers, and then working signs and wonders through them, not through Jesus, or Elijah, or Moses, but through ordinary people like you or me. (In fact, the Bible tells us Moses and Elijah were also ordinary people like you and me.)

He talked about being "baptized in the Holy Spirit," and showed me how John the Baptist had said Jesus would do this to believers. Then before returning to Heaven after His resurrection, Jesus had told the apostles they would receive the baptism in the Holy Spirit soon. On the day of Pentecost they did. In that moment one hundred and twenty ordinary people were transformed from the inside out. The early church was a place where miracles happened regularly.

Then Andy said, "God still empowers us through His Spirit. That's what happened when I prayed for Kenn." The truth was in front of me. I couldn't deny it. Kenn's eye *was* healed. No other reasonable explanation presented itself. The doctor had said it wasn't possible for the eye to have healed on its own over night.

In that moment I experienced a genuine faith crisis. I believed God had worked miracles in biblical times, but had never seen one or had any reason to believe He still did them in our day; what was I to think? Kenn's eye being healed could've been some freaky coincidence. It could've been a once-in-a-lifetime miracle; or it could be God still works in our day as He did in the early church.

Jesus' followers have argued and debated these matters down through the millennia. Some have said God is most assuredly still working in the same way today as He did then, because Jesus Christ is the same, yesterday, today and forever. Others explain the "age of the Spirit" is over and God works in us ordinarily through guiding our thoughts and actions as we learn and live His truth in the Bible. Those folks say while God does occasionally answer a prayer for healing, that's the exception, not the norm.

Those who don't believe in God would chalk Kenn's healing up to coincidence, or find some way to challenge that the event had occurred at all. I knew the healing had happened, but I wasn't sure what it all meant.

As I reflected on the situation, Andy asked if I wanted to be baptized in the Holy Spirit. That brought the faith crisis to a most personal level. If God does still act today as I had seen through Kenn's healing, then why wouldn't I want that kind of reality in my own life, to have the Holy Spirit empower me to be used to help others?

I said, "Yes," so Andy prayed for me and prayed for me, but nothing happened. I was confused. Andy told me when I was ready God would respond. I left a bit bewildered and overwhelmed by the whole experience. The events of the day kept rolling over and over in my mind.

That night as I was praying, I sat up in bed and said something like this: "God, I don't know about all this Holy Spirit stuff, but Andy seems to think it's pretty important, so if you're going to baptize me in the Holy Spirit would you just do it?" He did. While I could say much more about that, my point in sharing this dramatic sequence of events is to say I received a new direction from God as a result of all that took place in those couple of days. He made it clear pursuing fame and fortune was not my purpose.

God Got in the Way

The same night I experienced the Holy Spirit's power in my life, He spoke to me, as He has many times over the years in pivotal moments. He confirmed what Bernadine had told me when I was seven. God said, "I want you to serve me as a pastor."

I would like to tell you that in that moment I submitted my mind, heart, and will to Him, that I let go of my dream of becoming rich and famous and started planning to be a pastor.

I did not.

I rebelled against the idea instantly. I actually spoke back, "No way! I'm not going to be a pastor." I had many reasons why I wasn't going to be a pastor. Pastors aren't rich or famous. Anyway, why would I want to waste my life trying to get a handful of people to do God's will? Sort of funny, don't you think? I wasn't willing to do God's will myself, and part of my internal argument was it would be a waste of time to help others in that pursuit. I decided to continue pursuing the path to West Point. It seemed the clearest and most reasonable path to fame and fortune open to me. But the internal struggle had begun. I knew God was calling me to serve Him as a pastor, and I knew I wasn't going to do it.

The struggle continued for five years, taking many twists and turns. The amazing thing is God kept putting opportunities in front of me to test out the call to ministry. I was given the opportunity to lead a small youth ministry, to preach on a regular basis during college, to lead an adult Bible study. Every time I experienced one of those things, I sensed God's satisfaction and my own pleasure. As I took one detour after another trying to find my own way, or possibly to compromise with God, I never experienced the kind of fulfillment I did when I was doing something in the area in which He had called me to serve. More about that later. Right now, let's turn to one of God's most direct messages to me — a message that has changed my life for good in countless ways.

Finding Miss Right

In the fall of my senior year of high school, before I received the official notification about my appointment to West Point, I had talked with God about a wife. That might seem funny to you, because I was only seventeen, but as would have been true of many teenage young men in high school in those days, I had dated a couple of girls, and had found the experience less than fulfilling.

Knowing if I went to West Point, I would have to agree not to get married before completing my four years there, and being tired of the attempt to find "Miss Right," I told God something like this: "God, I don't need a girlfriend right now. In fact, I can't even get married until I've completed West Point, so when the right woman comes along, let me know. Thanks. Amen." (I've always had a straightforward relationship with God, and through the years prayers like that have been common.)

A month or so after I said that prayer, I was selected by Purchase Line to attend a high school forum in Indiana, PA. The purpose was to have two student representatives from each of the area high schools come together to discuss common problems and concerns in the schools and to work together to offer solutions. When the time came for lunch at the first meeting of the group, I saw a girl I had never met. God said, "That's your wife." It was the clearest message God ever gave me.

As I said, I had never seen nor met this girl. A few weeks earlier I had made it clear to God I didn't need a girlfriend for at least four years. Why would He point to this one and say, "That's your wife?" It made no sense, but I introduced myself. The girl's name was Nancy Fairman. She was from Marion Center High School. We ate lunch together and hit it off.

That was in October of 1974. I didn't attend another meeting of the forum until April of 1975. I saw Nancy at a couple of our basketball games that winter, and spoke to her when I did. I thought about her a lot, but never had the nerve to call her or ask her on a date. She probably already had a boyfriend, I reasoned. I also had the appointment to West Point, so what was the point of starting a relationship that was certain to be difficult, if not impossible, to continue?

The funny thing is the constant memory of God saying, "That is your wife," didn't fade. Finally, in April, I went to the last school forum meeting. It would be the last opportunity to ask Nancy to go on a date, and I was determined to do it. As soon as I saw Nancy, I knew my plan was in jeopardy. Marion Center had sent a substitute second representative that day. She happened to be one of Nancy's best friends. That meant Nancy would want to sit with her at lunch.

I had thought we would be alone during lunch — only Nancy and me. That would have made it much easier to ask her out. Now it was going to be the three of us. As we ate together, it became clear it is less than ideal to ask a girl out on a date, while one of her best friends is sitting beside her. I also had to leave the meeting early because we had a track meet that day, which presented another problem. Time was of the essence: if I waited much longer, I would miss my opportunity all together.

Thankfully, I was on Nancy's committee. When we got back for the afternoon session, I kept looking at my watch. I realized there would be no good time to ask her out before I had to leave. Mustering all of my courage, and in front of the whole group, I said "Nancy, would you like to go out with me on Friday evening?"

Without hesitation she said, "I have to ask my dad."

Right.

That's what I thought, *Right. She has to ask her dad.* I assumed she meant no, but she was too nice to say no in front of the group. (I would soon find out Nancy *was* too nice to say no in front of the group — that is, if she had wanted to say no.) She gave me her phone number and told me to call her that evening at 7:00 p.m. That seemed hopeful. Maybe she did have to ask her dad. It would soon become apparent she did, indeed, have to ask her dad.

Lee Fairman was a tough man when it came to his daughter. Many years later, when Nancy and I had two daughters of our own, I realized Lee was simply being a good dad. At the moment though he was the main obstacle to my going out with the girl I was sure God had told me was going to be my wife. (I guess if I were as sure as all that, I wouldn't have worried so much.)

It seemed to take forever, but 7 o'clock finally came. I called Nancy. She answered after the first ring. After we exchanged pleasantries, she said, "I can go out with you, but you have to come in the house and talk with my dad before we leave." When Friday came and I arrived at the Fairman home, Nancy welcomed me at the door. She took me into the den where her dad sat waiting. He stood up, shook my hand, and motioned for me to take a seat on the couch. I looked around the room and saw there would be nothing funny about this meeting. On the wall behind me were two stuffed bear heads. Across the room were a stuffed antelope head and a stuffed deer head. Behind Mr. Fairman was a gun cabinet filled with rifles and shotguns. I thought, *This guy likes to shoot things.* It wasn't a comforting thought.

As we sat there, Mr. Fairman asked, "Do you hunt?"

"No, sir I don't," I said, knowing that was the wrong answer.

"Do you fish?"

"No, sir. I don't." Wrong answer number two.

I felt the same way I had the day I faced that lefty's ninety-miles-per-hour fastball. It was 0 and 2, and I knew the hard curve was coming.

"Do you play sports?"

I breathed a sigh of relief and responded, "Yes, sir. I play football, basketball, and track at high school, and I play baseball in the summer." He asked me a few other questions. Then he told me I was to have Nancy back home by 10:00 p.m.

I didn't know it at the time, but when Nancy had asked her dad if she could go out with me, his answer had been a flat no. The school I attended didn't have the best reputation and Mr. Fairman thought I was probably a drunk or a drug addict, or at the very least that I was no good. Nancy's older brother, Ernie, had interceded and pointed out that Nancy would probably have noticed if I were any of those things. Mr. Fairman had acquiesced, but he was not convinced I should be permitted to be with his daughter. That opinion didn't change for quite some time.

One date led to another, and then to the prom. We were going steady. Then I graduated and the time for my departure to West Point neared. As the day approached, I became more and more certain I wasn't supposed to go. I knew I was supposed to be a pastor, but I wasn't going to do that either. One thing had become sure to me—God had, indeed, told me Nancy was going to be my wife.

No, Sir

July 7, 1975, came whether I wanted it to or not. That was my reporting date for West Point. Yes, I reported to West Point. Nancy made the trip with my parents to drop me off. My parents seemed proud. Nancy was encouraging.

I was neither proud nor encouraged. This was wrong.

I had known it from the moment I'd received the appointment, and long before that actually. I had known it from the moment God called me into the ministry, but had thought I could run away from the call, become rich and famous, and still follow Jesus in some manner—a manner more appealing to me.

After arriving at West Point and going through the first day, one thing was crystal clear—staying there would be a grave mistake. While I had the mental and physical aptitude to be a cadet and eventually a soldier, I had a call in my life to serve as a pastor, and no real interest in soldiering. I had allowed my parents' pride at my receiving the appointment and the affirmation of teachers—especially the one who said I couldn't get accepted—and many others, to sway my decision. There had been special recognitions in the local newspaper and at school. It was all quite exhilarating.

Eventually, I would come to realize only one person's affirmation matters—Jesus'. I wasn't there yet. At the moment the only thing I knew for sure, was I had to leave West Point, but it wasn't because I wanted to please God.

As the day progressed, the time came for all of the incoming cadets to sign the Oath of Allegiance. It was an impressive ceremony; all the cadets stood in line, and each one was asked, "Mr. _____ are you prepared to sign the Oath of Allegiance?" The proper answer was, "Yes, sir." When my turn came, and the question came, "Mr. Marshall, are you prepared to sign the oath of allegiance?"

"No, sir," I said. I was told to return to my quarters. Soon the two young men who would have been my roommates had I stayed joined me. They had been sent to help me change my mind.

The first said, "Why don't you stick around? It may not be as bad as you think."

"Why don't you send me a postcard and let me know?" I retorted.

The second said, "I wish I had your guts, but my parents would kill me if I left here."

"My parents aren't going to be happy either, but I have to do what I know is right for me," I said. When they saw they weren't getting anywhere, they left.

Soon, a knock came at the door, and it was a rising third-year cadet from West Point's basketball team. He had also been sent to try to convince me to stay. I had expressed an interest in playing on the team, which is why he was sent. The first thing he said was, "You're not making a bad decision. If I had it to do over again, I would never have come here." Now that was funny...

Next, I was sent to visit the cadet who would have been my platoon leader. He told me to sit down. Then he said, "Mr. Marshall, I've been here for three years and I've hated every minute of it, but when I get out of here, I'm going to be somebody."

I looked the young man in the eyes and said, "Sir, with all due respect, I am somebody right now." That response came from my heart and I believed it wholeheartedly, because of my relationship with Jesus. As I have reflected on that moment over the years, I've realized the courage to make that statement was not from me. Jesus gave me the courage both to say it, and to believe it. He had spoken those words to me.

The next stop was a visit to the base psychiatrist or psychologist. He was charged with determining whether I was making a rational decision. He asked me a few questions, determined my decision was rational and sent me to the base commandant.

The commandant asked me, "Young man, why did you come to West Point?

I said, "Sir, my parents wanted me to come and I didn't want to disappoint them."

"Aren't you going to be disappointing them now?" he asked."

"Yes, sir, I am, but I realized today I can't live my life for them. I have to live my own life."

He said, "Well, it took a man to walk in here, and it takes a man to walk out. If I can ever do anything for you, let me know." He shook my hand and walked out of the room.

Chapter 3

A Funny Thing Happened in a Nursing Home

What to Do?

By the time I left the commandant's office it was late. I was escorted to an isolated location on the grounds, where I spent the night. The next morning I was given the civilian clothes I had been wearing when I arrived, driven to the town outside of West Point, and dropped off there. Thankfully, I had been required to open a checking account at a local bank, because at the time cadets received stipends for attending the academy. I had made the required initial deposit of a hundred and twenty five dollars, which I withdrew and closed the account.

I walked to the bus station and considered my options. As I looked at the schedule, my first thought was, *I have enough money for a one-way ticket to California. I'll go there, establish myself and then call Nancy and my parents and let them know what I'm doing.* After all, if I were still at West Point, I wouldn't be permitted to talk with them for several weeks anyway. As I thought about that, some of the character traits that had gained me entrance to the academy in the first place surfaced. Realizing that running away was no response to my dramatic and last minute decision not to attend West Point, I bought a ticket to DuBois, Pennsylvania, and waited for the bus that would get me within a marathon of my home in Gipsy. (It is literally 26.6 miles from DuBois to Gipsy, which was as close as I could get by bus at that time.)

With the wait for the bus, and the transfer in New York City, it was late on July 8 when we arrived in DuBois. I booked a hotel room for the night, got up early the next morning, and started the trek home. Hitchhiking was common back then, so I walked and stuck out my thumb with each passing car. No one offered a ride. I walked all day, from morning until evening.

Family Reunion

By early evening I was about six or seven miles from home. As I continued walking, a green sedan passed. *Funny, that looked like my dad's car.* After passing me, the car skidded to a halt. It *was* my dad's car. Dad backed up and stopped next to me. He jumped out of the car and started pounding his fist on the roof.

In my entire life, I saw Dad cry only four times: Once when he had second and third degree burns on his chest; once when my mother died; once when he had his sixth heart attack; and once at that moment as he pounded his fist on the car's roof.

I got in. There wasn't much talking as we made the short, drive home. Once home, I went upstairs to my room. My mother talked with me briefly. I told her I was tired and wanted to take a nap. What I actually wanted was to die. My parents hadn't kicked me out of the house, which I had considered a possibility. After all I had thrown away a fully paid college education at one of the best and most respected educational institutions in America. I had thrown away the opportunity to serve my country. They were not happy with me, but at least they had let me come home. I drifted off to sleep. The twenty-mile walk, combined with the tense ride home with my parents, and my open-ended future had taken their toll.

Who Are My Friends?

A short time later, I woke up when I heard a light knock on my bedroom door. I went over and opened it. There stood Andy Weigand with a smile on his face. He said, "I want you to know two things: God loves you and I love you." He gave me a big hug. We talked briefly, and the funny thing is my attitude started changing. I believed what Andy said. I had believed God loved me when I sat talking with the platoon leader. God had given me the courage to remember I was somebody before I entered West Point, and would continue to be somebody even though I had left there and had no idea what the future would bring.

Nancy arrived not long after that. Mom had called her and she came over right away. She took me to her house, and to my surprise, her dad's response was positive. He had served in the Army and hadn't been too fond of the West Point graduates he had known. He told me he was glad I had come home. Nancy was glad to see me, too. I started feeling better.

A couple of days later, I stopped to see one of my best friends from high school. I knew he worked at a lumberyard in the area, and I thought maybe he could help me to get a job there, because his brother-in-law was one of the owners. When he saw me he asked, "What happened to your hair?" One of the tokens from my one-day stay at West Point was an extremely short buzz cut. I told him about my brief stay. He laughed and said, "Marshall, you're the only person I know who would drive 350 miles to get a haircut you don't even like!" That was the end of his concern about my not going to West Point.

It started to seem as if people weren't going to make a big deal about my short stay at West Point. I soon found that would not be the case with everyone. My true friends recognized while the whole process that had led me to West Point, and then to stay only one day, could have been avoided, it was a blip on the radar screen of my life. Others weren't so gracious.

You're a Failure

A week or so later, I drove to Punxsutawney to buy some clothes. I walked into a store and encountered a teacher from Purchase Line who had also been one of my coaches. When he saw me, he came over and said, "Marshall, I thought you were going to West Point?"

"I did, but I didn't stay," I said.

"You're a failure," he said. "You're never going to amount to anything. You had a fantastic opportunity to get out of here and make something of yourself. Now you've thrown it away." The words stung.

Part of me said, *I'm only eighteen. It's a little too early to pronounce me a failure.* Another part asked, *What if he's right?* Over the course of the next year or so, I realized a number of folks counted my life over because I had left West Point. They told me they were disappointed in me or that I was a failure or both.

Because I had been accepted to West Point so early in my senior year of high school, and was certain I would attend there, I hadn't applied to any other colleges. Now, I didn't know what I was going to do. The lumberyard where my friend worked wasn't hiring. I didn't know where to go to college or what to do next. I wasn't willing to throw in the towel and tell God I would study to become a pastor, but I was starting to wonder how the whole fame and fortune thing was going to work out for me.

I prayed about it, but every time I prayed seriously, it was obvious God hadn't changed His direction for my life. I thought about serving God as a pastor but every time I did I said, *No, way.* As I thought about it more and more, and prayed about it a little, I decided to become a doctor. After all, as a doctor I could serve people in Jesus' name, and I could probably still become rich and famous — at least rich. I applied to Grove City College, a small Christian college in western Pennsylvania. In my application, I noted I would also like to try out for the basketball team. I went to visit the school and was accepted for the January term of 1976.

That meant I needed something to do for the fall. Living in Gipsy, the job opportunities were limited. I found out the nursing home in Hillsdale was hiring so I applied to be a nurses' aide. Because I was going to become a doctor, I thought it might be good to be around folks who needed medical care. They hired me and I was assigned to work in the infirmary, the section of the home that housed the residents who needed some type of medical care or assistance with their daily routines. Many of them were on multiple medications. Some had experienced strokes. Others had what we would call

Alzheimer's or dementia today. It was challenging work, but I found it to be the kind of challenge that drew me closer to my calling — not as a doctor, but as a pastor.

Here's to You Mrs. Robinson

While I worked at the home, I was assigned to care for ten residents each day. My tasks included making their beds, feeding those who needed assistance, and attending to their other needs that arose throughout the day. The infirmary had three sections, and the aides rotated weekly from one section to the next. In the second section I met a client named Mrs. Robinson. When I started work Mrs. Robinson was in a wheelchair. She watched a lot of religious programming on television, and always held a well-worn Bible in her lap. I talked with her regularly, as I did with all of the residents in my care. One day I asked one of the nurses, "Why is Mrs. Robinson in a wheelchair? What's wrong with her?"

"Oh, there's nothing wrong with her, at least not physically," the nurse replied.

"You mean she can walk, but she doesn't?" I asked.

"She could walk when she came here, but at a certain point she stopped. Gave up, I'd say. She started saying she couldn't walk, and she hasn't since."

Mrs. Robinson became my focus. If she could walk, then I was going to help her walk again. During the weeks I was assigned to her section, I would take a little extra time to talk with her. I'd say, "Let's go for a walk, Mrs. Robinson."

She resisted at first. "I can't walk. I just can't walk," she would say.

I would tell her, "I bet you can. I know you can. I'll help you. I'll make sure you don't fall." This went on for weeks. On the weeks I wasn't assigned to her area, I still walked into her room once a day and asked her to go for a walk.

Finally, one day Mrs. Robinson said, "Okay. I'll try to take one step." I helped her up. She took one step. I moved the wheelchair forward and she sat down.

"Praise the Lord!" I said. Mrs. Robinson wasn't sure she would ever take another step, but the next day she took two, and the next day three. Before long she was walking up and down the halls. I went back to visit the home a few months after I started college. When I went to Mrs. Robinson's room she wasn't there. I asked one of the nurses where she was, hoping she hadn't passed away but also knowing it was a real possibility.

The nurse said, "Oh, she's living over in the 'penthouse' these days. She comes over here and visits the 'sick' people every day. She brightens up everybody's day."

Wow! How many Mrs. Robinson's are living in nursing homes all over the country? How many will never walk again, because no one takes the time to challenge and encourage them to do it? As I thought about it more and more, I realized a vital truth: One person can make a real difference in another person's life. No one can reach everybody, but everybody can reach somebody.

That realization became the impetus for the mission that now consumes my waking moments and has for many years: Sharing, growing and living the new life of Jesus Christ with the world — one person at a time. The funny thing is it was a 92-year-old woman sitting in a wheelchair who showed me the joy of helping one person take one step — literally in her case — from where she was to where she was going. Here's to you, Mrs. Robinson! Thanks for impacting my life by your willingness to trust me to help you take one step and then another.

A Good Idea — Not God's Idea

In January of 1976, I started Grove City College as a biology pre-med major. I tried out for the basketball team and "sort of" made it. After all, basketball tryouts had been held in the fall, and the season was in full swing when I stepped on campus for the first time. My roommate was another new arrival who was also trying out for the team. Dean came from Washington, D.C. He didn't follow Jesus, but he was an excellent basketball player, way better than I was. After a couple of weeks on the team, the coach came to me and said, "Chris, I've heard you're planning to try out for the baseball team. You're welcome to stay with us for the rest of the season, but you won't be getting much playing time. Baseball tryouts are next week. I'm not telling you what to do, but if you try out for the baseball team from the start you'll have a much better chance of making it." Message received. I left the basketball team and tried out for baseball the next week. The coach's advice had been right—I made the team.

The biology pre-med classes were tough, but I enjoyed them. I had always loved school and learning, and college was so much better than high school because all of the students in pre-med were serious about doing well. I liked the challenge and the environment—and it seemed the plan to become rich and famous while also helping others so God would be happy was going well. Then I went to church one weekend when I was home in Gipsy, and the pastor asked me how school was going. I told him it was going well.

He asked me what I was studying and why. I didn't know how to answer the why question, because it seemed to lack humility to say, "I'm studying to be a doctor so I can become rich and famous." Instead, I said something about doctors being paid well.

He said, "You know, I have a friend who is an audiologist. He makes a lot of money and he didn't have to go to college for eight years." That sounded good to me. I wasn't sure what an audiologist was or did, but I looked into it. I found out audiologists didn't make as much money as doctors, and audiology wasn't going to be a platform for fame, but the five-year education required to become one seemed preferable to the eight or more needed to become a doctor.

As I contemplated pursuing yet another career path, I knew it wasn't God's direction either. The funny thing was that mattered to me more and less at the same time. It mattered more because I continued to find that when I took on ministry opportunities I found great fulfillment. Folks also told me I was good at them. Several told me they thought I had missed my calling. It mattered less, because the longer I denied God's call in my life, the easier it became to keep denying it.

Once again I attempted to determine a path that would allow me to follow my way, while at the same time going somewhat in God's direction. I listened for God's input, but at the same time hoped He wouldn't give me any. I already knew His plan for my life, and still was having none of it. I thought about it being a pastor who had suggested audiology, and rationalized that maybe he was being guided by God because he was a pastor.

Many years later I would read Henry Blackaby's powerful book, *Experiencing God*, and understand the validity of his observation that God speaks to us primarily through the Bible, prayer, our circumstances, and other believers. Blackaby contended each method God uses is less reliable than the one before it. In other words, we always know the Bible is God's word and that He speaks to us through it. We generally know God is speaking to us in prayer when He does, although we can sometimes fool ourselves into believing God is speaking to us when we're merely speaking to ourselves. Our circumstances can point to God's direction for our lives, but sometimes a coincidence is simply a coincidence. Finally, when other believers tells us God has given them a message for us, it might well be He has. At other times, it might be they are playing the "God card" to get us to consider whatever it is they want us to do. My pastor didn't tell me it might be God's will for me to become an audiologist. He had mentioned the idea in passing. The more I considered it, the more it seemed like a good idea — not God's idea — but a good one nevertheless.

I checked into studying audiology at Grove City and found they didn't have the major. As I investigated, I found many of Pennsylvania's State System colleges and universities had speech and hearing majors, so during my one semester at Grove City, I applied to transfer to Indiana University of Pennsylvania, or IUP, where I would pursue a speech and hearing degree with a focus in audiology. My application was accepted, so in the fall I would be off to IUP.

One More Person at a Time

As I mentioned, Dean, my roommate at Grove City, had also come during the second semester and was trying out for the bas-ketball team. He made the team, and continued on it after I changed my pursuit to baseball. From the moment I met Dean I liked him. He was open about his disbelief in God and I thought, *What if God brought me here to help Dean come to know him?* Dean asked me a lot of questions about God so I eventually convinced him to read the Gospel of Mark. After he read Mark, I suggested he read Luke. One night he was lying on his bed reading his Bible. He stopped, interrupted my studying and said, "You know, if you believed this stuff it would change your life!"

The statement struck me deeply. I thought, *Yes, Dean. It would change your life.* Then I started thinking about my life. I was pursuing God's will in my life, but not fully. God had been changing my life since I was twelve. He had spoken to me clearly from time to time all of my life. Yet, in that moment I was sitting at a school ostensibly studying to become a doctor. I was in the middle of transferring to another school to become an audiologist even though I knew God had called me to become a pastor. I continued to focus on Dean instead of me. Maybe God did have me at Grove City for Dean's benefit. As the days went by and the end of the semester neared, I realized we probably wouldn't see each other again once I transferred to IUP.

My hopes soared when Dean came back from spring break. The first thing he said to me was, "Chris, you're never going to believe what I did while I was in D.C. on break!"

"What's that?" I asked.

"I told one of my friends about Jesus. Man, the dude needs Jesus." Dean said.

I said, "Wait a minute, did you trust Jesus as your Savior and Lord over break?"

"Oh, no," Dean said. "My friend's an alcoholic. He needs Jesus. If he doesn't make some changes in his life, he's going to die."

I was dumbfounded. Dean had realized his alcoholic friend was going to die if he didn't trust Jesus as Savior and Lord, and yet he hadn't realized he was going to die without Jesus if he didn't trust Him. In that instant, a thought occurred to me. I can't say God spoke it to me, but the thought was one I had never considered on my own during the entire first half of the semester. I said, "You know, Dean, when you think about it, you and I are roommates only because we both tried out for the basketball team. You made the team and I'm on the baseball team now, but we're roommates only because of our common interest in basketball. I've been thinking all this time that God put the two of us together so I could tell you about Jesus, but what if the devil put us together so you could draw me away from Jesus?"

Dean had been lying on his bed during the conversation. He bolted upright and said, "Chris, you just scared the hell out of me! I never thought about the devil before, but if all this stuff about Jesus is true, then the devil is real, too, because Jesus believed in the devil."

Exactly. I knew *all* of the stuff about Jesus was true because of the incident with Kenn. That meant not only did I know God — Father, Son, and Holy Spirit — is real; so is the devil. I had never considered the possibility that Dean might be there to tempt me, but the idea had a chilling effect on Dean. It didn't convince him to change. I lost touch with him after I transferred to IUP, but when we last saw each other, Dean was still an explorer. He was still considering whether Jesus' claims were true. He hadn't yet become a believer.

Over the decades since that semester, I've had many opportunities to meet folks and have them become part of my life whether for moments, months, years, or seasons. Each time, it struck me that God has given me the opportunity to meet them one at a time, to get to know them, and to share Jesus with them through my words and through my life.

Some have responded. Many have not. The point has been to be ready to share the new life I've received from Jesus with them, and to let Jesus do the rest. I've realized one of the dangers of being Christians is the tendency to insulate ourselves from the world, by surrounding ourselves with other Christians. I need to remember God offers us opportunities every day to share Jesus with one person at a time. It isn't up to us to convert people, but it is up to us to be Jesus' witnesses in each situation.

While that semester seemed to move me away from following Jesus' call on my life — after all, I did end up pursuing another major at another school the following fall, my experience with Dean initiated a lifelong desire to share Jesus with anyone who will listen, making certain as I share the truth of Jesus' salvation, I also share the love that sets Him apart from any mere religion.

Don't Pursue a Career in Public Speaking

In the fall of 1976, I transferred to IUP and pursued audiology with diligence. I liked the curriculum, and because most of the course work was in speech correction, I had the opportunity to gain an understanding of how speech and language develop, of their aberrations, and how they can be corrected. At the time, I didn't think that would be useful as an audiologist, and I might have been right. It was quite helpful, though, when I finally decided to stop running from God and become a pastor. I already had a firm foundation in

Jesus. My years as a speech and hearing student helped me build a foundation for my coming decades as a communicator and preacher.

It didn't seem that way at first. In fact, given that I have become a pastor — one who speaks in front of multiple hundreds of people every weekend — what happened in my junior year at IUP was funny. During the fall of that year, I ran for election as the president of the National Student Speech and Hearing Association (NSSHA) chapter at IUP. Somehow, I won the election. During my first meeting as president, I had to stand in front of all those speech and hearing majors and speak. While most of us are afraid of public speaking, it hit me right before I started speaking if I made even a minor mistake in pronunciation or stuttered for even a moment, everyone would notice. The pressure was too much. I stumbled my way through the evening, and did horribly.

After the meeting, the group's advisor said to me, "Chris, I hope you never get a job that involves public speaking." At the moment, she was right; at least she was right when it came to being in front of all those speech and hearing students. Then I thought about something — I spoke fluidly and confidently when I was doing something that had to do with God: leading a Bible study, preaching a message, just about anything. It still didn't hit me that God was confirming His call in my life, while I was steadfastly seeking to avoid it. The time would come when I would give in, but that evening at the NSSHA meeting, it didn't look like there was any use because I couldn't communicate in front of a group anyway.

Paying the Bills

During the first summer after college, I got a job at the lumber-yard where my friend worked. It gave me fifty-two hours of work each week during the summer months. I had lived at home during my first year at IUP, and continued living there while working at the lumberyard that summer; that made saving money quite easy. Tuition was less than $500 per semester (Yes, less than $500 per semester.), and I was able to pay as I went through college. That fall I moved to an apartment in Indiana, continued to work at the lumber-yard part-time, and ate most of my evening meals at Nancy's house.

During my second summer after college, I was working at the lumberyard when Frank Fairman, one of Nancy's cousins stopped to pick up supplies. He was the foreman of his dad's carpentry crew. "Uncle" Lowry Fairman built new homes. As I loaded Frank's pick-up with supplies he asked, "How much do they pay you to work here?"

"$3.00 an hour," I said.

He said, "I wouldn't get out of bed for $3.00 an hour."

Without thinking, I said, "Why don't you give me a job that pays more?" The funny thing is, he did. He told me I could work for him in the evenings and on Saturdays. He would pay me $5.00 per hour to start. Back in 1978, that was pretty good money for a college stu-dent. I continued to work at the lumberyard during the day and for Frank in the evenings and on Saturdays. It was a challenge to work seventy to eighty hours per week, but it did more than pay my bills; I discovered I loved carpentry work. I loved the sense of accomplish-ment of starting with nothing and then seeing a house with a new room, or tearing off an old roof and putting on a new one. Frank

and I were both competitive so we turned everything into a com-
petition—who could lay the most shingles, who could drive a nail
with the fewest hits. (Yes, we actually pounded nails with hammers.
We didn't have nail guns in those days. In fact, after several months
of working with Frank, because I'm left-handed and I drove lots of
nails, my left forearm was much bigger than my right. Nancy called
it my "Popeye" arm.)

After a couple of months, Frank told me to ask his dad for a
job. Being that Frank was the foreman of his dad's crew, I figured it
would be an easy job interview. I was right. I drove over to Lowry's
house and asked him if I could come to work for him. He told me
he would start me at $3.50 per hour. (I'm good at math and calcu-
lated in my head that forty hours a week at $3.50 per hour would
be a cut in pay from working fifty-two hours a week at $3.00 per
hour, because twelve of the hours were paid at time-and-a-half.) I
told Lowry that and he started me at $4.00 per hour and within a
few months bumped it up to $5.00. I now had a job I loved, two of
them actually, because I kept working for Frank in the evenings and
on Saturdays, and learned skills that have helped me throughout my
life. I didn't see at the time how God's hand was at work in this job
switch, but as you'll see later, the carpentry skills I learned opened
doors I never considered at that moment.

Miss Right to Mrs. Marshall

As I moved through college, Nancy and I became closer. From
my second year of college on, I spent more and more time at her
house. Nancy's dad warmed up to me a bit over time, although all
of his life he called me "Marshall." I realized eventually that was

a Fairman characteristic of Lee's generation. Lee had nine brothers and two sisters. The brothers called everybody by their last names or nicknames, even each other. By December of 1976, I knew for sure Nancy was the one for me. Lee was a traditional kind of man so I decided to ask him for permission to marry Nancy. One evening in mid-December, I was scheduled to pick Lee up after work in Indiana. I would ask him on the ride home. As I drove Lee home, he talked about his day and asked me about mine. I couldn't summon the courage to turn the subject to asking him for permission to marry Nancy. Finally, we were only about a quarter of a mile from their house, when I said, "Lee, I'd like to ask your permission to marry Nancy. We won't be getting married right away, but I wanted to ask you before I ask her." I knew God had told me Nancy was going to be my wife. I was pretty sure that by this time Lee had figured out I would eventually be asking him if I could marry her.

He was more than ready when I asked. For the next forty-five minutes we sat in the car in the Fairman's driveway as Lee gave me a lecture, sermon and seminar all wrapped into one about how important marriage is and about how young people today don't take it seriously enough. He told me if I did marry Nancy there wasn't going to be any divorce. He talked about having children some day, and how you have to be there for them. Then he talked about his marriage to Margaret, and how he had done some things right and some things wrong. I'm sure there was much more. The funny thing is at the end of the conversation, Lee said, "Yes."

I popped the question on Christmas Eve. Nancy and I drove from her house to Gipsy to spend the evening with my family. I had the ring in my car, and I didn't know for sure when I was going to ask her, but I figured I would know when it was the right time.

(Guess you can see why I need the book *Life Planning*.) What I hadn't counted on was the snow that had been falling gently as we left Creekside would be falling much harder as we neared Gipsy. As with most rural areas, there are many ways to get from point A to point B, and I had chosen the shortest route. The problem was the shortest route included a long uphill incline in the road at one point. My 1972 Chevy Vega couldn't make it through the unplowed snow. I turned around and headed another, longer way. It was long before the time of cell phones, so my parents were probably starting to get worried by how long it was taking us, but our "fun" was only beginning.

When we were about two miles from Gipsy, we passed under an electrical transformer. We had driven about a hundred yards beyond it, when it exploded. It looked like fireworks going off in the middle of the snowstorm. If I had been thinking of anything other than getting that little Vega to our house, I would've stopped and popped the question in the glow and sparks of that transformer's fireworks. Getting home was my only focus. When we finally pulled into our driveway, we were both relieved to be there. Thinking quickly, I realized I didn't want to ask Nancy to marry me in front of my family. That would've been too much like asking her out for the first time in front of the entire committee of high school students, so I asked her right there in the car. It wasn't nearly as romantic as I hoped it would be, but she said, "Yes!"

I was a junior in college at the moment and Nancy a sophomore, so we didn't set a date for our wedding for a while. On April 14, 1978, we decided to get married exactly one year from then. It was a long year. We were both working, and during the summer we both worked long hours. Lee had decided to build a "retirement home" on the hill above their house that year. He told me if I helped him build it, Nancy and I could rent it when we got married. That sounded great to me. Who wouldn't want to live in a brand new house as newlyweds? My carpentry skills were already coming in handy. We completed the house in early 1979, so I moved in before we got married, and Nancy was only seventy-five yards down the hill. Everything was moving in the right direction. One thing kept bothering me though—I couldn't get the idea of God's call to become a pastor out of my mind.

For some reason I didn't talk with Nancy about it. Given that I was planning to be married to her for the rest of my life, you would think I would have at least mentioned it to her. She knew I liked doing church work. I had been doing youth ministry with some of the young people from her church and another church in the area. I had led some adult Bible studies and classes at her church, where I had decided to become a member. I had also been preaching at various local churches most weekends, and she had accompanied me most of the time, often playing the piano in the churches where they had no one to accompany the music. But in the midst of all of that, I had started to consider going to law school—yes, law school. I had done well academically and had inquired with one of the professors in the political science department whether he thought I would be able to get into law school, given my background as an education major in speech and hearing. I had taken a business law class and Pennsylvania school law. When he saw my grade point average, he smiled and said, "I'm sure we can get you into a law school."

I've often thought about how amazing Nancy is to have married me in the first place. I had never officially told her I felt called to be a pastor. I was very up front about being a committed follower of Jesus, as was she, but from the day we had started dating, I had switched from one possible profession to another. I was going to go to West Point and eventually become a lawyer. Then I was going to become a doctor. Then I was going to become an audiologist. Now, I was considering becoming a lawyer again. The common thread in all of those jobs was income potential. Becoming a pastor was not a vocation with income potential. Because Nancy was still going to be a junior when we got married in April, and I still had a semester of college to go in the fall in order to graduate, we had some time for me to make a final determination so I didn't mention it.

On April 14, 1979, Miss Right became Mrs. Nancy Marshall. As we stood stating our vows to each other, we thought everything would be wonderful. As most young couples do, we assumed everything was going to work out because we loved each other. The funny thing is, it has, but it hasn't been anything like we had it pictured as we stood at the front of Center Presbyterian Church in Creekside, PA, looking lovingly into each other's eyes. Given that we were both students, and our economic situation was tight, we took a short honeymoon locally, and then came home and got right back to studies and work. We enjoyed being married, and as with nearly all marriages the first few months were fun. That would change relatively quickly.

Chapter 4

A Funny Thing Happens in Marriage

Honey, I'm Going to Be a Pastor

It wasn't more than a month or two after we were married when I changed my mind about my vocation again. This time I decided to go with the vocation to which God had called me five years earlier. "Honey, I'm going to be a pastor," I said to Nancy. She took the news well on the surface. In fact, Nancy has been a trooper all through our married life. We had no idea what it was going to mean for me to be a pastor. I didn't even know which denomination I would serve as a pastor. Having grown up as part of Gipsy Christian Church, and having joined Center Presbyterian Church after I started dating Nancy, I wasn't sure which, if either, denomination was better for me to serve.

I called Andy Weigand and asked for his advice. He told me about the Christian Church seminaries that were available. Then he said, "Don't apply to more than two seminaries."

"Why?" I asked.

"Because you're going to be accepted wherever you apply," he said.

Over the next several months, I investigated seminaries, spoke with pastors and prayed a lot. The funny thing is many times God had given me clear instructions or at least clear indicators in my life to that point—this was not one of those times. I thought once I had finally said yes to God that He would show me everything I needed to do, that He would speak more clearly to me than ever before. He didn't. Eventually, I decided I would enter the Presbyterian Church's process and become a candidate for ministry with them.

During my times of extensive prayer, God had made one thing clear to me, or at least it seemed God was speaking, "You can make a difference." I thought of Mrs. Robinson and how my perseverance had helped her to regain her independence and then to serve others herself. I thought of Dean at Grove City, and how I had been able to show him that Jesus is real enough that he witnessed to one of his friends about needing Jesus, even though Dean wasn't yet ready to follow Jesus himself. I thought of how many times I had been able to help a young person through youth ministry. I thought of the affirming comments I had received from the members of the small churches where I had preached. I knew the Presbyterian Church was struggling, that I wasn't close to 100 percent behind the denomination's theological and social positions, and that they didn't even believe in the current work of the Holy Spirit, as I understood and experienced it.

When it came time to be interviewed to become a candidate for ministry, I was asked why I had decided to become a Presbyterian and to enter the ministry in the Presbyterian Church when the denomination was going through so many challenges and divisions. I responded when one disagrees with the direction of a local church or denomination, one has only two choices: 1) leave and find another one; or 2) stay and work to bring it back to faithfulness. I said I was choosing to stay and work to bring it back to faithfulness. That met with rousing approval from the pastors and elders gathered that day. I was approved unanimously as a candidate for the ministry. I didn't realize then that after identifying doors number one and two, and choosing door number two—staying to work to bring the denomination to faithfulness—that I would work for that goal for a season of seventeen years. Eventually door number one would lead me in another direction. Funny how God works....

Choosing a Seminary

Eventually, Nancy and I narrowed the seminary search to two—Gordon-Conwell Theological Seminary in Massachusetts, and Princeton Theological Seminary in New Jersey. We visited each of the seminaries. While my theology was conservative and much more aligned with Gordon-Conwell, Nancy and I agreed Princeton offered better opportunities for her to find a job, as well as being closer to home. In addition, the presbytery had told me if I attended Gordon-Conwell, I might have to attend a Presbyterian seminary for an additional year when I had completed my three-year Master of Divinity program. Once I finally decided to be a pastor, my goal was to become one as soon as possible. I didn't want to add an additional year to the process. I applied to both seminaries, but Nancy and I had decided Princeton was our first choice. While we prayed about the decision, God didn't seem to be answering so we decided to let the circumstances be God's answer.

When we received word that I had been accepted at both schools, we accepted Princeton's offer of admission, but asked for a one-year deferral before starting. I had accumulated a small debt in my final year of college, not from college itself, but because I had bought a new car. We wanted to be debt-free when we entered seminary, so we decided to work for another year before moving to New Jersey. The deferral was granted.

Because this book is dedicated to pointing out the funny ways God has worked through my life, I need to point out that the year we waited before starting seminary was filled with ministry opportunities — more preaching on a nearly weekly basis, the opportunity to lead more Bible studies, and the initial phases of working through my candidacy in the Presbyterian Church. At the same time, I had decided to do carpentry work for the year of waiting because it would be the best way to make the most money to pay off the car and to save for seminary.

The challenge was I was no longer working for Lowry and Frank. They laid me off the previous winter, and I had taken a teaching job in January of 1980 as a speech therapist. It was a long-term substitute position as I took over for a woman who was on maternity leave. That meant I was employed from January through May. The potential of continuing to work the following year was there, but I was a short-timer as a speech therapist, and carpentry work would provide more income. Frank and Lowry didn't have work for me, but through my church connections I was able to get a job with another contractor, Gary Huber. It seemed like a "God thing," and it was. I was able to add some skills I didn't have before, because Gary's specialties were painting and roofing. My skills also helped Gary get into some areas he hadn't worked before, so we experienced mutual benefits from our year together. When it came time to leave for seminary, Nancy and I had paid off our debt, and even had a little money in the bank.

God at Work

Because I was going to be a full-time student again when we moved to Princeton, Nancy needed a full-time job. She had spent the previous year teaching at Purchase Line, my alma mater, and was interested in finding another teaching job. She sent resumes to a number of districts in New Jersey and eventually got a few interviews. A couple of weeks before I needed to report to Princeton for school, she and her mom went to New Jersey so Nancy could have a final interview with one of the schools. They would also be able to get an initial look at our apartment in the seminary's student housing complex. Nancy was hired to teach in a district about an hour's drive from Princeton, which was truly a blessing. When she went to the apartment for the first time, it was not such a blessing. As she walked in and turned on the light cockroaches scattered everywhere. Yes, cockroaches. Nancy has always practiced orderliness and cleanliness in her life, and once we were married in ours. This was not good. Thankfully, the cockroaches were temporary residents. The exterminator had sprayed the apartment on the floor above earlier that day or week, and the roaches had taken up residence with us. Another visit from the exterminator corrected that, and the apartment was livable before we moved in. No one can say whether the roaches would have been a deal breaker for Nancy, but I'm glad we didn't have to find out. On the day I started classes as a student at Princeton, Nancy had a teaching position, we had an insect-free place to live, and all was well with the world.

Or so it seemed.

One of the funny things Nancy and I have experienced over the years is when life gets overwhelmingly hard, God shows up. I don't mean those times always get easier. I don't mean the bad situations always get better. Sometimes they have. Sometimes God has made us tougher, or helped us to see the good aspects of the difficulties, or given us the strength to hold on.

Sometimes He has done miracles.

Shortly after Nancy started her teaching job, it became apparent the situation was not what it had seemed in the interviewing process. It wasn't that it was hard, or that the students didn't care, or that she didn't feel she had any support from the administration, it was all of that and more. By the time we approached the end of her first semester of teaching and my first semester at seminary, Nancy said, "I can't do this anymore."

I said, "You need to quit."

"We have to have this income," she said.

"God wants us to be here, and He'll see you have a job," I said. You need to give your two-week's notice." This discussion went on daily. Finally, Nancy had come to the end of her rope. She agreed. We drafted a resignation letter, and Nancy left for school with the letter in hand. She would work until the end of the semester.

After that?

We had no idea. The semester was ending, Christmas was coming; as we looked to the New Year, Nancy needed a job.

Nancy and I don't recall the precise timing of what happened next. Sometime after Christmas, I was sitting at home in our apartment studying for finals while she was teaching her last few days of school. The phone rang and when I answered, the person on the other end asked to speak with Nancy. I told him Nancy wasn't home and asked if I could take a message.

He said, "Nancy applied for a teaching position in our district last summer, and we have an opening for the next semester. I was calling to see if she is still interested." I nearly did a back flip. I told him I would have Nancy call later that afternoon. Remember, this was still long before cell phones so I couldn't call Nancy at work. I had to wait all day for Nancy to come home so I could tell her that God was at work big time, that He was answering our prayers.

When she came home, Nancy was excited, but in her reserved way. She pointed out that she hadn't even been offered an interview for sure. I said, "But you had an interview with them before. You know God is behind this." She called the man, and she got the teaching position. You might not believe in God. You might think this was one more happy coincidence. I believe it was God showing us He cares about His children. To be sure, the position lasted for only one semester, but it was a timely answer to a great moment of need in our life together. Nancy loved the job after having struggled all through the fall. Nancy hated to leave the position when the semester ended. Yet, it showed us in a moment when we had trusted God enough for Nancy to turn in her resignation without any assurance of another job except that we knew God would provide one; He was there for us and He did.

During the summer ahead, I would be able to work, and Nancy would have time to find another job. She did. It was a job she held for the rest of our time at Princeton. She worked in the housing office at Princeton University, where she made some good friends and worked on one of the first IBM PC's on the market. That process helped us to see God was, indeed, for us.

We have worked our way through many challenging situations over the years. When we have, we always remember the times when God has shown Himself to us so clearly. None of those times are clearer than that moment when He provided Nancy a job after she had stepped out in faith and tendered her resignation from an untenable position when she had no other job prospects before her. At its best, life is harder than most of us imagine because we live in a fallen, sinful world. Thankfully, we who know Jesus Christ personally serve a God who is faithful and who is always with us through the good, the bad, and the even worse. That the extraordinary God of the universe reveals Himself to ordinary people like us still amazes me every time He does it. I hope you have experienced moments like that. If you haven't, Jesus wants you to experience them. He has been waiting for you and will wait for as long as it takes; because the funny thing is He extends grace to those who seek it, no matter how long or short the time before we seek it.

Only Greek Makes Sense to Me

We've all heard the expression: It's Greek to me. It means we're confused. We don't understand. The funny thing is my first year at Princeton, most of the time Greek was the only thing that did make sense to me. I entered seminary as a conservative follower of Jesus who had experienced the fullness of the Holy Spirit in the healing of my brother, and in my own personal experiences of being filled by Him. I had heard God's voice and experienced His hand on my life many times. I soon discovered I had entered a world that was vastly different from all that. I found it extremely unnerving.

Living in New Jersey was literally like living on a different planet from Gipsy, Creekside, or even Indiana, Pennsylvania. The pace of life was at light speed compared to anything we had ever experienced. As I've noted, Nancy's job didn't go well from day one. My classes at Princeton challenged me more than I had ever been challenged before. It wasn't so much the academic challenge, although the sheer volume of the daily reading assignments was daunting. What bothered me the most was some of my professors didn't seem to take biblical realities as realities at all. They spoke of demythologizing the Bible. They spoke of spiritual realities as if they were merely psychological phenomena. I left the lectures in many of my classes confused, but not in Greek class. Thanks to Mrs. Stephens, my eighth grade English teacher, I understood the parts of speech in English quite well. I knew how to diagram sentences. My training in speech and language development had equipped me to learn another language with different pronunciations. When we started learning paradigms and declensions I was ecstatic. While Greek has irregular verbs, as does every language, for the most part Greek was a constant in a widely inconsistent time.

At the end of the first week of Greek class, I walked up to our instructor, Dr. Elizabeth Edwards, and said, "I want to be one of your teaching assistants when I'm a senior."

She didn't know me yet so she asked, "How much Greek have you had?"

"One week," I responded

She smiled broadly and said, "Okay. Why don't you complete this year, take a couple of Greek exegesis courses next year, and then check back with me about being a TA when you're a senior."

I smiled back at her and said, "Okay, but I'm going to be one of your TA's when I'm a senior." And I was. The thread of sanity through my seminary days was Greek. As I learned the paradigms, and the nuances of the language, which remained constant, it built a foundation for other courses. It was also a safety net when those other courses seemed to be pulling the platform out from under me. It still seems funny after all of these years to say Greek was the only thing that made sense to me during my first year of study at Princeton, but it's true. Thankfully, I found encouragement in another arena, through a means God has used throughout my life to show Himself to me—a pastor, mentor, and friend.

A Pastor, Mentor, and Friend

While many first-year students at Princeton chose not to work in a church on the weekends, I had worked in churches on weekends for the last couple of years of my time at IUP, and in the year between college and seminary so I decided to go ahead and apply for a field education placement. I applied at three churches. At the first couple of interviews, the pastors didn't talk much about Jesus. At the third interview, I met an immediate brother in the Lord, Arthur Pace. We hit it off right away, and when I received a call to serve as the Field Education Student at Garwood Presbyterian Church where Arthur served as pastor, I accepted enthusiastically.

I learned so much about ministry that year, but much more important, Arthur encouraged and challenged me to become more than I thought I could be. One of the practical truths Arthur taught me the very first day I worked with him has stayed with me ever since. He said, "Chris, if you watch me in the year ahead, you will see me do a number of things well, and if you learn from them, you will become a more effective pastor." Then he continued, "You will also see me do many things poorly. I have many weaknesses. In those moments if you discount me, or fail to learn what not to do, you will miss the opportunity to learn. You can always learn whether from a good example or a poor one."

I have sought to remember that wise counsel, particularly when I have been exposed to poor examples. It's so easy to discount those who offer poor, bad or even evil examples, but we can always discover lessons to be learned. The best students learn from every example, not only the good ones. Arthur was a gracious man. He was fairly young, only a few years out of seminary himself when I started to serve under his leadership. The church he served had many folks who were older than he, and some were unkind in their assessment of his leadership. He treated them with grace. I had seen the same response many times from Andy Weigand, the pastor from whom I had learned so much as a teenager in Gipsy. Arthur challenged me to remember that ordinary people are valuable to God. He told me that because I generally absorbed his lessons quickly and was ready to move on to something else. I was always looking to learn the next thing.

Arthur helped me to see our task as pastors is not always to be quicker or brighter than everyone else, but to help as many people as possible to know Jesus as Savior and Lord, and then to help those who do know Him to grow to full maturity. It is often a slow, arduous and even tedious process. I have too often forgotten that lesson over the years, as my tendency is always to forge ahead, to press on to the next endeavor. But now more than three decades later, one of the best affirmations I can hear from someone is, "I didn't understand that before, but now it's clear to me because of how you explained it." I've heard it called putting the cookies on the bottom shelf. Theologians would probably call it incarnational ministry, because when we serve one another in the truth and love of Jesus demonstrating His patience as we do so, others have the best opportunity to see and know Jesus. Incarnational ministry means putting *flesh* to Jesus in the way we live our own lives, so others might see Jesus in us and come to know Him too.

When ENFP Lives with ISTJ

During the second year of seminary, Nancy and I found ourselves disagreeing with each other about many things. Then we started arguing about them. We seemed to see "back to back" on many issues, from little things like how to squeeze the toothpaste, to big things like why I hadn't told her I was going to become a pastor when we were dating. Living 300 miles from home—on what seemed like a different planet—didn't help. Money pressures were common. I studied so much that we couldn't spend a lot of time together. The honeymoon was definitely over.

As I thought and prayed about this matter, asking God to fix it, a thought occurred to me: During the process of becoming a candidate for the ministry, I had been required to take the Myers-Briggs Type Indicator, and Nancy had taken it as well. While we didn't understand everything about the personality inventory, we knew we were four letter opposites: I was an ENFP and she was an ISTJ. She liked order and structure. I liked spontaneity, and chaos was fine with me. I liked being around lots of people and felt energized when I was. She needed time alone after being with people. I was always buying things on impulse, and liked surprising Nancy with gifts. She didn't like surprises and wanted life to be predictable. At one point, it got so hard we sat down and looked at each other; both of us were exasperated by life in general, and by each other in particular.

In that moment, an idea came to me. I said something like this, "Nancy, remember that personality test we took? It says I'm an ENFP and you're an ISTJ. That means we're 180 degree opposites, so we will always be at each other like this." I demonstrated by taking the fingers of my left hand and bouncing them off the fingers of my right hand. Then I said, "Or we could complement each other like this." I demonstrated by interweaving the fingers of both hands. That was the beginning of a long and on-going effort to learn from each other and about each other. It didn't get easier in an instant, because we were and we are still basically different people. But that moment was pivotal for us. In that moment we committed to our marriage vows, and have worked at them through the many trials, temptations, and tests that have come over the years. We have both fallen short of our expectations of each other and of ourselves. The funny thing is while it has taken decades to get to where we are, we have experienced so many blessings, because we have made that commitment, not the least of which has been the benefit of being able to see life from the opposite perspective of our own through all of these years.

These days I often tell people, "When Nancy and I agree on something, I know it's right because we see things so differently. When Nancy and I disagree on something, Nancy is usually right."

90

That's no joke. It's usually true because her personality is so much more detail-oriented than mine that she has the facts of a situation together before she makes a decision. There are rare occasions when I'm right, too. The key truth to take from these few paragraphs if you're married or are in a significant relationship that might lead to marriage is this: personality differences *will* come out over time. That is not a "deal breaker." If God has brought you together, then nothing is a deal breaker, provided you let Him be in charge of your relationship and speak into your lives when times are hard.

Spoiler alert: Times will be hard far more often than you might imagine.

The Memorable Dr. Willis

During my years at Princeton, many of my professors challenged me through their lack of belief in what I considered basic biblical truths. For example, one of them took me aside and put his arm on my shoulder after my first paper in an introductory course in the Old Testament. He did so to tell me that he had once believed as I did, which at the moment meant he had once believed Noah's ark actually existed. He told me that after three years at Princeton, I would no longer believe such things because they were myths written to demonstrate truth—not to record actual events. To say I was shocked would be a massive understatement. Thankfully, I was already under Arthur Pace's tutelage, and was learning to learn from all examples both good and bad, true and not as true. The funny thing is it was a professor whose theology I never actually determined who said the most memorable things during my time at Princeton. His name was Dr. Willis.

The first thing I remember from Dr. Willis's introduction to theology class was his definition of faith. To this day, I don't know whether it was his definition or someone else's, but I have always remembered it — *Faith is an informed trust, not a nice gullibility.* Indeed. Those who do not believe in God often contend it is gullible to do so. Some reasons for believing in God *are* simply a nice gullibility. But one need not hold such a flimsy faith. While it isn't the purpose of this book to make a case for the reasonability of trusting in Jesus Christ as Savior and Lord, I have found over the course of my life that God's intervention is one, substantial reason for holding such a faith.

Is there a more informed trust than experiencing the hand of God in one's own life? I remember hearing Dr. Willis's definition of faith and immediately thinking, *Yes! That's right!* Faith is so much more than a nice gullibility. The informed nature of one's trust in God can be extensive. It's a matter of investigation, and a willingness to trust the truth even when the truth seems to go beyond the natural. After all, because faith in a God who created everything out of nothing requires a belief in the supernatural, that which goes beyond the natural, it is only reasonable to assume we must investigate as thoroughly as we can when something occurs that seems to go beyond the natural, such as an eye healing overnight, or a man rising from the dead.

The next memorable truth from Dr. Willis came in the form of an illustration he used when he was talking about sin. He said Presbyterians hold that humans have a "tendency" toward sin. Dr. Willis wanted to demonstrate that tendency. He took a chair and placed it beside his lectern, stood upon it, and said, "In a moment I am going to say, 'Now.' Remember that moment." After giving us that instruction, Dr. Willis started leaning to the left. At a certain moment, the moment at which the pull of gravity was greater than Dr. Willis's ability to stay upright, he started to fall to the floor. In that instant, he shouted, "Now!" As he gathered himself off the floor after his dramatic illustration, he said, "The 'tendency' toward sin is as compelling as the force of gravity. We cannot escape it."

I remembered my own discovery of the "tendency" toward sin when I was five and had attempted to shoot my mother. While many might have disagreed with Dr. Willis, I have always remembered his illustration, and have experienced that tendency toward sin many, many times. The best hope each of us has to overcome that tendency is to recognize its pervasive nature, and to call on God to fill us with His Spirit daily in the name of Jesus Christ.

A couple of weeks before graduation, Dr. Willis told us that in our three years at Princeton we had learned a whole new vocabulary, a whole new way of thinking in many areas of our lives. He told us when we went out to serve in churches we could use that language to confuse people and to show them how intelligent we were. Then he said, "But, if you are always hitting over everyone's heads when you talk, it is not necessarily a sign of intelligence. You may just be a poor marksman."

That statement struck me, because it coincided with Arthur Pace's comment about making sure I not outpace the ordinary people I serve. To be sure, all of us are far more ordinary than extraordinary, especially when God is the standard. But sometimes when we have gained a different vocabulary because of our studies or experiences, or when we have accomplished something others have not, we might find it easy to think we are better than or even superior to them. Thanks to Arthur, Dr. Willis, and most of all, Jesus, I have learned the best way to get the message of God's salvation in Jesus across to others is to be as clear and simple as possible. After all, at the end of the day, I don't want to be a poor marksman when the target is helping someone to know Jesus Christ as Savior and Lord, or helping someone to grow up to be more like Him.

The final memorable message from Dr. Willis came on my last class with him. At the time, one of the most popular shows on television was *Hill Street Blues*. It was a police drama, in which the personal and professional lives of a particular precinct's officers and detectives were shown in compelling ways. One of the notable lines from the show was Sergeant Phil Esterhaus's warning at the end of roll call each day. As he dismissed the group, Sarge would say, "Let's be careful out there." In closing our class for the final time, Dr. Willis said, "If I could alter a line from Sergeant Phil Esterhaus, as you go out into a world desperate for the good news you have to offer them, 'Let's *not* be careful out there!'" Wow! I had watched the show; I knew the line. The simple addition of the word *not* made all of the difference. So many people spend their entire lives being careful not to offend anyone; not to get hurt; not to be noticed. Dr. Willis reminded us Jesus makes all of the difference. If God has taken the risk of entering our world in the man Jesus Christ, and of dying on our behalf, then we need to *not* be careful out there. We need to make sure everyone hears, everyone knows, and every possible person experiences the blessing of knowing Jesus as Savior and Lord. I've always remembered that benediction. When the opportunities have come to take the easy way or the shortcut, I've remembered Dr. Willis's admonition to *not* be careful out there. It has saved me from so many safe calls over the years, and has given me the opportunity to hear God's voice, because when you're taking the well-worn path

94

it's seldom needed, but when taking a new direction, God's voice is essential.

Have you ever known the safe way was the wrong way in your life? I hope you took Dr. Willis's advice to *not* be careful out there. Even now, if your tendency is to take the safe, easy or conventional way, and you hear God calling you to a different path remember to *not* be careful out there because God's voice is often clearest when we're not walking the well-worn path.

There's Nothing of Interest

I learned quickly while at Princeton that Presbyterians are fond of abbreviations, acronyms and acrostics. (They also like alliteration.) As I entered my senior year, I learned of SPONs. These were Senior Placement Opportunity Newsletters. The SPONs were printed regularly and offered students the opportunity to find out about churches that needed pastors. I had already determined I would be going to a church as a solo pastor, I would not be moving to a city, and I would not serve in a large church right away. Even though I had submitted to God's call in my life to become a pastor, I was still in the habit of putting boundaries around what that meant. When the first SPON was published, I got one, brought it home, scanned it, and saw all the opportunities were as assistant or associate pastors in larger churches located in cities, so I pitched it in the garbage can. When Nancy came home from work that evening, for some reason she looked in the garbage can, saw the discarded SPON, and asked, "What's that?"

"Oh, that's a SPON, a Senior Placement Opportunity Letter. There's nothing of interest in that one," I responded.

Ignoring my comment, she looked through it and said, "What about this church in Cincinnati? It looks like it might be interesting."

I said, "It's an assistant pastor job. I don't want to be an assistant pastor."

"Well, maybe you should at least interview with them. They're coming here to Princeton and it would be a good experience to have an interview," she said. She was probably right. I decided to go ahead and interview with the church. It *would* be good experience.

Why Did I Wear My Pirates' Sweater?

The day of the interview came, and as I got ready I put on a pair of dress slacks, a dress shirt and my Pittsburgh Pirates sweater. The sweater was gray with the Pirates' emblem embroidered over the heart. Nancy asked me whether I ought to dress up for the occasion, but because I wasn't interested in the position, it seemed the Pirate sweater would be fine. Ordinarily, I would have invested time in prayer over such an important meeting, but I saw it as nothing more or less than an opportunity to improve my interviewing skills so I didn't give it much thought.

About five minutes into the interview, I realized I was more than interested in the position. It seemed God was opening a door to a ministry I hadn't even considered. The position was mainly youth ministry, which I loved, but it also offered the opportunity to work with adult and children's ministry, and promised more preaching than the typical assistant pastor position. Suddenly, I wondered why I had worn my Pirate sweater. I spent the rest of the interview trying to sit in such a way that my right arm hid the emblem from view.

When I got home that afternoon and told Nancy I liked the church a lot, she said, "I told you it looked interesting." The pastor had said they would be calling for second interviews in two to three weeks. It was fairly early in the first semester of my senior year so I felt no sense of urgency, but it was exciting to think I could receive a call to serve in a church before the semester ended.

The pastor did call for a second interview, which we scheduled over the Thanksgiving break. Nancy and I drove to Cincinnati after spending Thanksgiving at home in western Pennsylvania with our families. I had bought a new sports coat for the interview, not wanting to wear the Pirates sweater again. The interview went well, and before we knew it, we were being offered a call to serve as the assistant pastor of Crestview Presbyterian Church in West Chester, Ohio. We still had the ordination process to go through, and the approval of the Cincinnati presbytery, but before the end of the first semester of my senior year, we already knew where we would be going after graduation.

I Need a Computer

As I entered my final semester at Princeton, the pressure was off because we already knew we were going to serve Crestview. As classes began, I noticed a few of my classmates had purchased "personal computers." Remember, this was 1984. Personal computers were a new fad. IBM had come out with their PC, which was extremely expensive. Compaq was entering the market, along with Commodore and others. I had used a typewriter since seventh grade because my penmanship was so horrendous. I told Nancy if I could get a computer, I was sure my work would improve. As usual, she looked at it practically, and said, "If you want a computer, you're going to have to get a job to pay for it." I took her up on the challenge. Because I already had a church, I needed only to pass my classes, not ace them. I wasn't working in a church on the weekends, because I was Betty Edwards' teaching assistant in Greek. The question was what kind of job I could get that would fit with my class schedule, and wouldn't require a car, because Nancy used the only car we had to drive to work.

The answer came quickly. At the end of our street was a business called A-1 Limousine. I walked there to see whether they were hiring drivers. The dispatcher gave me an application and told me to complete it. Another guy sat near me waiting to be interviewed. As I completed the form, a door opened. A sign hanging over the door read "President." The man who came out looked first at the guy sitting near me, then at me. He said to me, "Come in here." I went. He said, "Are you a seminary student?"

"Yes," I replied.

He said, "Do you have a valid driver's license?

"Yes."

"Do you have a black suit?" he asked.

"No, but I can get one."

He said, "When you do, come back and you can get started."

I said, "I didn't even finish the application."

"That's okay," he said. "I know you'll do a good job. I've hired other seminary students. You're honest. You show up for work, and you can keep your mouth shut when our customers open theirs. And you live within walking distance, right?"

"Right." I said. The president walked me out to the dispatcher and told him all I needed was to finish the application and get a black suit. Then I'd be back and he could schedule me with one of the other drivers for training. I finished the application, gave it to the dispatcher and went home. Wow. That was even easier than getting hired by Lowry. When Nancy came home, I told her about the job "interview." We both saw God's hand all over that, but some would say it was simply one more coincidence.

It sure was funny in any case.

That evening we ran into another "coincidence." We went to the local mall, walked to the first men's clothing store we saw, and there in the window was a sign that read: On sale! Below the sign was—you guessed it—a black suit. We found one that fit for $89, and the next day I went on my first training run with A-1 Limo. After one more training run, I was on my own. The job was perfect. It paid $5 per hour plus tips, which were usually good. I could read for my classes as I waited for planes or trains to come in, and if they were late, I got paid to study for class. It was a win-win situation.

In no time, I was able to get my computer. It was a KayPro IV-Plus 88. I don't remember much of what that means. I do remember they advertised it as a "portable computer." It weighed 27 pounds and looked like a metal suitcase when you carried it. Its claim to fame was it had a 360K floppy disk and could store "dozens of pages of information." It was a blessing, because now I could hone my papers to how I wanted them to be instead of saying, "Good enough," after typing and re-typing a couple of times. I learned with that first computer that computers don't save you time. They make it possible to improve constantly because nothing is permanent until you hit print.

Think about this: I started in the ministry officially in 1984. I started using a personal computer at the same time. It was cumbersome and I bought a replacement for it in a few years, but I have served my entire thirty plus years in ministry with a computer as the primary means of composing. That has meant from day one I could compose better material, store it and revise it over time, and eventually share it with others in ways that so many people before me and even after me have not been able to do. Some have come to see the massive technology and social networking of our day as tools of the devil. The fact is, they're tools, and as with all tools they can be used for good or evil. We get to choose, and the choices have become much more complex over the years. The key is to continue choosing to use the tools available to us to honor God, and to advance His purposes.

Chapter 5

A Funny Thing Happened at the Hospital

The Move

After Crestview extended the call to serve, the process of becoming their assistant pastor was a matter of checking off a long list of items from the denominational to do list. The process went smoothly, and before we knew it, we were loading the moving truck for Cincinnati. I would like to say God spoke to me or to Nancy and me often during the process, but He didn't. After receiving the call from Crestview, I was freed up during that final semester at Princeton to focus on classes and to work my job at A-1 Limo. I also played a lot of Ping-Pong with Andy Ross, my best friend at Princeton. He had also received a call to serve a church early so we enjoyed lunch together daily, and then engaged in some serious Ping-Pong matches. We knew our days together were numbered because he was headed to Yakima, Washington after seminary, so we invested as much time together as we could.

As we drove from Princeton to Cincinnati, Nancy and I looked forward to moving on with our lives. Nancy had been supporting us for three years, and while her final two years of working at Princeton University had paid the bills, it wasn't what Nancy wanted to do for the rest of her life. We both looked forward to finding our new roles, and I was eager to start working at Crestview. One of the best aspects of my start at Crestview as I saw it, was the senior pastor, Dr. Rich Doerbaum, was going to be taking six weeks of vacation and study leave soon after I arrived. I would have the opportunity to preach every week, and to be in charge of the daily routine, along with the challenges of getting established in a new church. While some might have seen the task as daunting, it sounded like a lot of fun to me.

The night we moved into our apartment, we thanked God for the new opportunity and went to bed looking forward to the next day. As it turned out, the next day started a lot sooner than either of us had anticipated. Shortly after we went to bed, the phone rang, which seemed odd, because only a few people other than our parents had our phone number. We had finished a couple of weeks on vacation with our parents the day before so it didn't seem likely they would be calling. They weren't. Rich's son, David, was calling to tell me that a member of the church had suffered a heart attack and wanted to see the pastor. He was at Bethesda North Hospital. Could I go right away, because Rich had left for Florida? I said I would be glad to go, but I had no idea where Bethesda North was located.

Baptism by Fire

David gave me the directions. I got dressed, jumped in the car and headed to Bethesda North. When I arrived, I went to the emergency room and told the nurse in charge I was a pastor from Crestview and was there to visit a parishioner. She took me to meet the family, the man's wife and three sons. I didn't know it at the moment, but we would become extremely close over the next few days. Karen, the wife, told me Bob, her husband, was in his 40s. She said they had not been permitted to go back to see him. The boys: Todd, Scott, and Mark ranged in ages from middle school to recently out of high school. The concern on their faces was evident. Eventually, the nurse told me I could see Bob. I could tell by his expression that he thought he was going to die. I introduced myself and he said, "Pray for me." I did. I didn't stay long. I spent the night with the family. Bob made it through the night. He made it for much longer. That experience meant that for the rest of my time at Crestview, and for long afterwards, Bob, Karen, and the boys were some of our closest friends.

From that experience, and so many like it, I have learned something important about God and His word — Romans 8:28 is true. God *does* work in all things for the good of those who love Him and are called according to His purpose. God showed me that night that sometimes the best ministry is simply being there. I believe the prayer I offered for Bob was used by God to make a difference. I also believe my being with the family meant as much to them as anything in that difficult time. It bonded us together in ways good times cannot. We have shared many good times together since then, but it has been the painful times that have sealed the relationship. The funny thing is we always want good times. We always want life to be easy, and yet the difficult times are the ones when our faith grows, and we experience God's grace most deeply.

I Don't Want to Work

After we settled in at Crestview, Nancy told me she didn't want to work for a while. She wanted to stay home, take care of our apartment, and be a housewife. That was fine with me. Nancy had been sacrificing her own desires for our entire married life. I was glad to give her the opportunity to do what she wanted. A few weeks of being home all day showed Nancy that maybe she didn't want to be at home all the time. Nancy had always enjoyed arranging flowers, and had even had a part-time job in a florist shop while we were in seminary. She said, "I want to take a class in flower arrangement." Again, that was great with me. I wanted Nancy to do what she felt called to do. She took the course and got a job working for a florist. After a few months Nancy told me that while she loved arranging flowers, doing it for a living was taking the enjoyment out of it for her. She wasn't sure what she wanted to do, but she wanted to try something different.

Rich's wife, Kathy, was a real estate agent. Nancy thought about studying for her real estate license because she had always enjoyed various aspects of the home. Her degree was in home economics education, and one of her favorite assignments had been to design a home, complete with wiring diagrams, floor plans, and elevations. I had cooperated with her on the project because at the time I was working with Lowry and Frank and had a working knowledge of building processes. Selling real estate appealed to Nancy more from the aspects of helping people find the homes they wanted and could afford, as well as helping folks who were going to sell their homes prepare to do so. She took the courses, passed the licensing exam and started working in real estate. She enjoyed her work, and soon became quite successful at it.

One of the most challenging aspects of that period in our lives was selling real estate and working in ministry are both vocations that can and will consume all of your time if you let them. Soon we were letting them. We were both working long hours and found ourselves seeing little of each other. We were usually tired when we were together and our relationship started to suffer from all the hours we worked. I have heard often over the years that sometimes when a person works in the church he or she can equate church work with God's work, but the two aren't always the same. During those years, I often confused the two, and chose church work over God's work, which would have meant investing more time with Nancy. We live in a world that gives us confusing and contradictory signals about what is important in life. That era of our lives showed me that it never goes well when we think work, even God's work, is the be all and end all of life. Even God rested on the seventh day of creation, and modeled the necessity for us to live in a rhythm of work and rest. The funny thing is, in this case I didn't learn to imitate God's example quickly or easily. I hope you'll take a moment right now to ask yourself, "Does work have an appropriate role in my life, or is it too much or too little a part of me?" If you don't have a daily job that keeps you occupied during the week, is there anything that you are permitting to take the place of God and your other important relationships? It's vital that we take time on a regular basis to stop and ask ourselves such questions, and then to let God speak into our lives.

Pack Your Bags

After I had been at Crestview for a short time, I realized I was in a vastly different culture than either that of Gipsy or Princeton. The people of West Chester were wealthy. They might not have thought so, but most were upper middle class folks, nearly all professionals, and most on the fast track to success or slowing down from it. Some of them undoubtedly wanted to be rich and famous. Having realized that in my role as pastor I was to speak God's truth in love into people's lives in ways that would impact them the most, I always asked God what to preach about the next time I had the opportunity to preach. The response was clear on one of those occasions, "Tell the people to put me first." As I thought and prayed about that, I knew precisely what that meant—I was to lay it on the line, to tell everyone that unless Jesus was first in our lives, it didn't matter who or what was second.

I needed to help folks see when Jesus said, "Seek first the Kingdom of God and His righteousness and everything you need will be added to you (Matt. 6:33)," He meant He was to be the center and focus of everything. I wrote the message and was excited about the opportunity to preach it. Then a disturbing thought struck me: *This could upset a lot of people.* After all, I was saying we needed to put Jesus before our jobs, our money, our families—before everything. The night before I was scheduled to preach, I told Nancy, "Pack your bags. After the folks hear this message, the session (the church board) is going to vote to get rid of me." That is not exactly what a husband—pastor or otherwise—ought to say to his wife, when they've moved to a new area to start a new job, but I knew I hadn't always been up front with Nancy about what I was thinking vocationally over the years. I wanted her to be the first to know my message was challenging and that folks might be offended by it.

I prayed a great deal that night and asked God to empower me to preach His truth in love. That prayer has become so important to me over the years. The theologian Reinhold Niebuhr once said speaking the truth in love is justice, but speaking the truth without love is injustice. The idea of speaking the truth in love comes directly from the fourth chapter of the Apostle Paul's letter to the Ephesian Church. In any case, throughout my ministry my goal has been to speak Jesus' truth, in His love, and to trust that Jesus will be glorified and will use that truth and love to change people through me. The next day, I preached with every ounce of passion and conviction I possessed. I preached the truth that Jesus deserved to hold first place in our lives, and while my zeal was high, I genuinely loved the people of Crestview and wanted them to understand the stakes of living a life less than fully devoted to Jesus. After each of the worship services people came to me and said, "Thank you. That's what we needed to hear." I was amazed. I told Nancy. She was relieved.

The next time I prepared to preach, I sensed God's leading to challenge everyone again. I told Nancy, "Pack your bags. This message is going to push people to the limit." Again, the people affirmed the message. The next time I had the opportunity to preach, the boldness to preach was there again and I told Nancy, "Pack your...."

She interrupted me. "I'm not packing my bags. You're preaching what God wants you to preach and the people are responding to Him." She was right. I learned through those early experiences that preaching the truth in love is *always* God's way, and God's will. Over the years at various churches, I've thought about lightening up a bit. Each time I'm reminded while "lite" beers might taste great and be less filling, there's no place for "lite" messages in Jesus' church. Jesus did not endure a "lite" flogging or a wishy-washy crucifixion. He gave everything, so we must listen for His voice and then speak His truth in love. That's true whether it's standing in front of a church family preaching a message or speaking one-on-one with a person at school or work. The funny thing is when we do that people respond. They come to know Jesus. They grow up to be more like Him. It always starts with being willing to put Him first.

Can You Come?

One time early in my ministry at Crestview, my phone rang a few minutes before 10 p.m. When I answered it was a woman I didn't know. Her name was Jane, and she told me that she and her family had recently started attending Crestview. She had been diagnosed with a melanoma on her face, and was leaving for Johns Hopkins Medical Center the next day for treatment. She wanted to know whether I could come and pray with her. I was leaving for Dallas the next morning for a weeklong youth seminar. The timing wasn't optimal. I've discovered over the years that the timing of people's needs fitting into my plans is seldom optimal. This was one of those moments when the need was both important and urgent.

I asked whether anyone else was with her. Jane told me her husband and two teenage sons were with her. I got the directions, jumped in my car and headed to their home. As I drove I prayed, "God, what did I learn at Princeton that will help me deal with this situation?" Silence. I thought about it and realized that might actually have been God's answer — nothing. Then I said, "God, what is there in Your word that will help me with this situation?" Immediately,

James 5 came to my mind. When I arrived, the family introduced themselves to me. I asked if they had a Bible, and they brought me one. I turned to James 5:14-15:

> Are any of you sick? You should call for the elders of the church to come and pray over you, anointing you with oil in the name of the Lord. Such a prayer offered in faith will heal the sick, and the Lord will make you well. And if you have committed any sins, you will be forgiven.

I asked Jane if she had any oil, and she brought me some cooking oil from the kitchen. We anointed Jane with the oil, and then the dad, two sons, and I laid hands on her. I asked God to heal Jane in the name of Jesus. Jane had told me the melanoma was on her cheek, and tests had shown "tentacles" had spread throughout the cheek area. The doctor had told her she would have a one-in-five chance of living five years. After we prayed, Jane asked me, "What should I do now?"

"Go to Johns Hopkins tomorrow and do whatever they tell you to do. I'll check back with you next week." I promised to pray for her each day, and left. I prayed for Jane that week and wondered what happened during her time in Maryland. The next Sunday Jane came up to me at church. She wore a tiny, circular Band-Aid on her face, and she was smiling. I asked, "What happened?"

She said, "When I got to the hospital they did some pre-surgery tests and they couldn't find any cancer. They saw a small spot on the X-rays so they made a tiny incision, and found a few cells. They told me I don't even need chemotherapy or radiation. I only have to go back for checkups every six months." I was amazed. This was even better than Kenn's eye being healed, and God had used Jane's husband, sons, and me to do it. Once again, God had spoken clearly.

Over my several decades as a pastor the results of prayer have not always or even often been like that. I have prayed for others with cancer who have died. I have prayed for folks with torn ligaments and they've been healed, and others who have received healing through surgery. The key is to pray in faith. That's what James told us to do. I recently read when we ask God for something He always answers. The author, Daniel B. Lancaster, said the answer might be: no; slow; grow; go. In other words, sometimes God doesn't give us what we want because He knows what's best. At other times, the answer comes slowly because we need to develop patience. At still other times, the answer comes slowly because we need to grow in some area of our lives. Sometimes God says, "Go." (Or "Yes," but that doesn't rhyme with no, slow, and grow.).

While the way he put it seems a little cheesy, I agree with his perspective. We don't pray to coerce God to do what we want. We pray because God has told us to pray. He has told us to bring our needs to Him. He has told us to praise Him and to confess our sins to Him. As we pray we don't know what God's answer will be, but we can know God will answer because He loves us. I am old enough to know God has been gracious enough not to give me everything I've prayed for over the years because in retrospect I've prayed for some seriously stupid things. At other times, I have no idea why God hasn't given me what I've asked for because I've prayed in faith, have asked over and over again, and know what I'm asking for is consistent with His will. At the end of the day, He is God. His will is the best will, and I'm learning the times when He answers prayers as

He did our prayer for Jane are a great blessing because they remind us that He is able to do more than we can ask or imagine, and they call us to deeper faith and commitment to Him.

No Problem

I said earlier that Henry Blackaby has written God speaks to us through His written word, through prayer, through circumstances, and through other believers. One of the best examples of God speaking through other believers during my time at Crestview was through a man named Mert Bomgaars. Mert was an elder in the church, and Nancy worked with his wife, Ruth, selling real estate. I didn't know Mert well the first time I turned to him with a problem, but what I learned has stayed with me ever since. I was in what I considered to be a serious jam. When I first came to Crestview we had 800 members, but only $400 in the youth ministry budget for the entire year. After I'd been there for six months or so, we had spent the $400, but needed an additional $400 for an upcoming youth event. I don't even remember why I went to Mert for advice. It was undoubtedly a prompting of God. In any case, I sat down with him and said, "Mert, I have a problem."

"What is it?" he asked through his teeth as he puffed on his pipe.

I said, "We need $400 for a youth event, and we've already spent everything in the youth budget for the year."

Mert started laughing. Laughing. I asked, "Mert, what's so funny?"

He took his pipe out of his mouth, looked me straight in the eyes and said, "I have two dead kidneys. If I don't get a kidney transplant I'm going to die. *That's* a problem. Always remember

this: Any problem that can be solved with money isn't a problem."
To make his point, Mert got out his checkbook, wrote a check to the
church for $400 with youth ministry in the memo line, handed it to
me and smiled.

I've always remembered that moment. I've always remembered
any problem that can be solved with money isn't a problem. That
advice has helped so many times over the years when it seemed
money was the only thing that would keep a ministry I was leading
from moving forward. I would remember Mert's statement, his
laughter, and start to pray.

Mert had an expression, "No problem." He said it a certain way
that made you sure there was no problem after all. A couple of years
after Mert's initial lesson about what does and does not constitute
a problem Nancy and I had the opportunity to buy our first house.
The house needed a lot of work. We didn't have any money for a
down payment. We would have to offer the sellers a lease purchase
agreement. I went to Mert to ask his advice. He heard me out and
then asked, "What's the problem?"

I said, "Mert, I don't know if we'll be able to make the payments.
We might lose the house."

"You don't have a house now, right?" he asked.

"No, I don't."

"So the worst thing that could happen is you lose the house and
you have to live in an apartment. You're living in an apartment now,
right?" He looked at me with a smile.

Long pause.

We made the offer. The couple went for the lease purchase. With
my carpentry skills and the commissions from houses Nancy sold,
we converted the house into a $15,000 profit several years later when

Nancy and I moved back to Pennsylvania. That gave us a real down payment for a house there, but that's getting ahead of the story. The point is time and time again Mert helped me to see many of the "problems" I thought I had weren't problems at all. They were opportunities. Some were opportunities for others to be used by God to help. Others were opportunities for God to use the skills He had given me to help. Sometimes they were simply opportunities to trust God and watch Him work.

No matter what the outcome, when you put God first, there is no problem because the worst thing that could happen is we end up in Heaven with Jesus. I don't make that comment flippantly, but as a statement of faith. We serve a God who will supply all of our needs according to His riches in glory, as the Apostle Paul put it. We must remember, though, the same Apostle Paul who reminded us of that truth went through unimaginable difficulties in the course of his life, in order to serve Jesus and to tell individuals and multitudes that Jesus is the only way to the life that is truly life. I thank God often for Mert Bomgaars, and for so many people like Him over the years who have reminded me that God often speaks and works through ordinary people because at the end of the day, that's all He has. God working in ordinary people who trust Him to work through us means "no problem."

Time for Children

Nancy and I had thought about having children during our seminary years but for some reason we weren't able to have any. We prayed and asked God to give us a child but no answer came. Then one day, something happened that, in retrospect, was somewhat similar to what the doctor had told my mom before I was born—some medical advancements had occurred that might make a difference. We had decided we weren't going to take heroic measures to have children. God could bless us with children if he wanted to do so, or we would live without them. Either way would be fine with us. At a routine visit, Nancy's doctor told her that he wasn't proposing anything dramatic but it was possible a hormonal imbalance was keeping her from conceiving. She took a supplement for a few months, and she got pregnant. Talk about an answer to prayer. We had been praying for years for God to bless us with a child and now Nancy was going to have one.

The joy was short-lived.

In a matter of a few weeks after we found out Nancy was going to have a baby, something went wrong. She started to have some bleeding, and then some pain. On February 15, 1988, we lost our first baby to a miscarriage. This is a book about how God shows up in ordinary people's lives, about how He speaks to us in many different ways. As I sat in the emergency department waiting room that morning, knowing Nancy had probably lost the baby, but not being permitted to be with her, I started to pray. As I prayed, a scene from the life of King David came to mind.

King David had been a great king of Israel, a man after God's own heart. But one day David made an incredibly bad decision. He decided to commit adultery with a woman named Bathsheba. As a result, she became pregnant. David attempted to cover it all up by having Bathsheba's husband Uriah, who was a soldier in David's army come home, spend a couple evenings with her, and then attribute the pregnancy to him. David's problem worsened, though, because Uriah was a man of integrity. He wouldn't go home to be with his wife while his fellow soldiers were at war. Finally, David sent Uriah back to the battle with a message for his commander. The message was for the army to put Uriah on the front lines and then to draw back so Uriah would be killed. The commander followed David's orders and Uriah died.

We're told as a result of this sequence of events, the child born to David and Bathsheba was sick. It lived only a short time and then died. All during the week of the baby's sickness, David fasted and prayed. When the baby died, David got up bathed and ate. His servants didn't understand David's response. They couldn't understand why David had fasted and prayed until the baby died, but then the moment the child was dead, David got up, bathed, and ate. It made no sense to them. David told them that as long as the baby was alive, he thought, "Who knows? Maybe God will hear my prayer." But after the baby was dead, David realized he could do nothing. Then David told the servants that the baby would no longer come to him, but that one day he would go to the baby.

Those words comforted me greatly in that moment. They were God's words to me. David might not have been speaking of eternal life when he said one day he would go to his baby. He might have meant nothing more than one day he would die, as the baby had. I believe David was saying what I also believe; "I will see my baby one day, because he is already in Heaven." I believe we will see our baby one day, because she is already with Jesus, and one day we will be too. That is the promise for all who trust Jesus as Savior and Lord. You might be thinking, "That isn't much comfort." No, in the moment it wasn't, but it was enough. I pray if you have ever gone through such a time you have known the small comfort of God's presence, and the promise that one day we shall be with Him, too.

Hopeful Grief

As God's timing would have it, a week after Nancy's miscarriage, I was scheduled to preach on 1 Thessalonians 4:13; a passage in which the Apostle Paul told the believers in the Thessalonian Church that those who died before Jesus returned would get to be with Him. The first century believers thought Jesus was returning in their lifetimes so when folks started dying before Jesus returned, they had a legitimate concern that those who died might miss out on experiencing life with Jesus. Paul addressed this matter, and made a powerful statement about the nature of our grief as Jesus' followers. He said, "We don't grieve as the rest of people who have no hope."

The message was extremely hard to write and to preach because of how raw our grief for our lost baby was, but it was also a powerful message because it was born out of the reality of that loss. Some of Jesus' followers tell us we ought not mourn when fellow believers die. After all, they are with the Lord and are far better off than we are. That is absolutely true, but the Apostle Paul reminded us we who remain here still suffer loss when a loved one dies. To be sure, if the loved one has lived a long and productive life in the Lord, it is easier to say good-bye than in the case of a miscarriage or of a young person's death, but facing a loved one's death is never easy. When we love someone, we grieve when we lose him or her. It doesn't matter whether the loss comes through death, divorce, moving away, or any other type of separation.

We don't grieve as those who have no hope—but we do grieve. The funny thing is, when we grieve the loss of those we love in the hope of Jesus Christ, it actually moves us to a healthier place than when we pretend everything is okay, or when we forget the reality of our future reunion with those we have lost. We experience tension in the reality that our loss is our loved one's gain. That tension will remain until the day we experience the gain of dying to this life and being with the Lord, too.

Many times over the years, events have occurred in my life, my family's life, the church family's life, or the world around us, when I have turned to the scheduled Scripture and topic for the week ahead, and it has spoken directly to that issue. In those moments, I have been amazed at how clearly our extraordinary God has prepared us for those events. After I preached the message on Hopeful Grief many folks in the Crestview church family came to me and told me how much comfort they had received through it and how timely it had been for them. God often communicates His comfort, encouragement, even challenges to us through the source we call His word, the Bible.

Out of the Mouths of Babes

About six months after Nancy and I went through the miscarriage, Nancy became pregnant again. This time all went well with the pregnancy and on June 11, 1989, Abby Elizabeth Marshall joined the Marshall family. It didn't make up for the loss of our first baby, but it certainly brought us great joy. God has spoken to me so clearly over the years through Abby, and later Emmy Margaret, our youngest daughter, who arrived on December 7, 1993. Sometimes God has spoken to me directly through our daughters — as the time when Abby was about four years old and I was throwing a tantrum or doing something that wasn't measuring up to the standards I had set in my messages. She looked at me and said, "Daddy, there's no sense preaching about what you aren't going to do!"

No, there is no sense preaching about what you aren't going to do. I was convicted by the accuracy of Abby's words, and the message sank straight to my heart because the messenger was so cherubic. King David tells us in Psalm 8 that God has ordained praise from the mouths of infants and children. I have experienced that so often over the years. While our daughters are adults now, and aren't following Jesus' ways as they did so faithfully when they were children and teens, many of the messages God has given me over the years have come directly through them. I hope you have experienced this means of God's communication in your life, either through your own children or through the comments of other children. Little wonder that Jesus said we would never enter the Kingdom of Heaven unless we turn and become as children. Their innocence, their perception, their love, and their trust are all qualities that allow us to hear God's voice, as well as to receive it in our lives.

I have often said Jesus reminded us we must be childlike, not childish if we want to experience the reality of His Kingdom, which would certainly mean hearing His Father's voice. The childlike qualities mentioned above open us to the reality of the miraculous, the good, and the eternal. Childishness is the selfish two-year old throwing a tantrum because she didn't get what she wanted. Many times when I have heard God's voice, it was because of my openness to hearing and receiving what God was saying, as a child would receive the message of a loving parent.

It Is Time for You to Leave

Shortly after Abby was born, Nancy and I sensed it was time for us to move to a church where I would be the pastor rather than an associate pastor. My five years at Crestview had demonstrated one of my gifts was preaching, and my leadership skills sometimes clashed with being in a position where my leadership was only in a few areas of the church rather than having responsibility for the overall vision and ministry. Being part of the Presbyterian Church USA in those days, the process was to compile a Personal Information Form (PIF) and send it to the denominational headquarters to be matched with churches whose Church Information Form (CIF) showed similar emphases for ministry.

As would be true in many vocational settings, I didn't want to announce I was planning to leave to the entire body of Crestview too soon; this would hamper the work or ministry I was doing there. One of the first people I told about my plans to leave was Mert. He said, "I was wondering when you were going to leave. If you ask me, you were ready a couple of years ago." At first I was offended, thinking Mert wanted to get rid of me. Then I realized all Mert was saying was my season of being an associate pastor was over. It was time to move on to the next season. I told Rich of my plans, and started preparing for that next season of life as a senior pastor.

To be frank, I wasn't even sure I would continue to be a pastor. While much had been good about serving at Crestview, the lingering thoughts of fame and fortune had never left. A chiropractor friend had suggested I might want to go back to school and get my degree in chiropractic. His practice was booming and in a few years he was going to need an associate. As I sat around his swimming pool imagining such a life, it seemed extremely attractive. As I prayed about it, I finally decided to give the ministry one more try before going back to my original dream of fame and fortune.

Why Does Everybody Want Me?

At that time, in the Presbyterian Church, USA (PCUSA), opportunities for churches seeking pastors and pastors seeking churches to meet Face-to-Face were offered periodically in various regions of the country. One such Face-to-Face event was offered in Toledo, Ohio, shortly after we decided it was time to move on from Crestview. The process for the Face-to-Face was each pastor received the CIFs from all of the participating churches, and the participating churches received the PIFs of all of the participating pastors. Pastors were given the opportunity to select their top four churches, and were guaranteed to have interviews with at least two of those top four churches during the day of the event. If time permitted, additional interviews could be added. I submitted my requests and waited for the response of the event's planners.

One of the churches attending the Face-to-Face was from Cincinnati so they contacted me and asked whether I would be willing to interview with them before the event, because that would free up an interview spot at the actual Face-to-Face for both of us. I agreed. The interview went well. The church had a lot to offer a young pastor who was seeking his first call as a senior pastor. It was a growing, ethnically diverse congregation, and their vision for ministry was similar to mine. It seemed as if it could be a good match.

When the packet came from the Face-to-Face organizers, I found I had been given my top two choices from the list of attending churches, as well as three other interviews. As I walked in that morning, a couple folks from a church that was not on my list walked over to me and said, "You're Chris Marshall, right?"

"Yes." I responded, wondering who they were and how they knew who I was, because my PIF didn't include any photos.

"We know you don't have us on your list of churches, but would you be willing to stay afterwards and talk with us briefly?"

I was honored they asked, and accepted the opportunity. As the day progressed, each interview went well. Churches from Michigan, Ohio and one from Pennsylvania had sent representatives to the event. A larger church from Columbus would have been the best opportunity from a purely professional standpoint. They were offering an excellent compensation package. They had a staff that I would have the opportunity to lead. They were approaching 1,000 people in membership, and in many ways would have been similar to Crestview. The church from Pennsylvania was much smaller, but from the moment I sat down with them, I sensed this was the match God had for me. We addressed all of the formal interview questions, but the interview moved beyond formality to a comfortable, enjoyable atmosphere. At one point, we had been laughing together several times, and an event administrator came in to ask us to please keep it down because we were disturbing the interviews going on in the adjacent rooms.

Each interview, including the one in the parking lot at the end of the day, went well. The way the process was supposed to work was pastors and churches would follow up with one another in their own timing. At the end of one interview, the church committee said, "We know you're the pastor for us. We understand you need some time to think and pray, but we hope you will come and be our pastor." In the days that followed, all but one of the churches called with invitations to come for a second interview. It was a bit overwhelming. I said to Nancy, "Why does everybody want me?"

I felt affirmed and encouraged to continue in the ministry with so much interest from that handful of churches. That being said, I had driven home the night of the Face-to-Face and told Nancy, "We're moving to Pennsylvania."

"You mean a church offered you a call already?" she asked.

"No, but they will," I said. She wanted to know how I could be so sure. I told her I just was. It was one of those times when I knew God was speaking. Sure enough, in a couple of days, I received a phone call from the Pastor Nominating Committee of Glade Run United Presbyterian Church in Valencia, Pennsylvania. They wanted me to come for a second interview. Nancy and I were eager to at least consider moving back to Pennsylvania. With Abby now part of our family, it would be great to be within an hour or two of our parents. We arranged the second interview, and Nancy, Abby and I headed to Valencia for what turned out to be a defining moment in our life together. The second interview confirmed what the first had made clear — we were a good fit as pastor and church. At the end of the interview, the committee told me they were ready to extend a call for me to be their pastor. I told them Nancy and I needed to pray about it, and we would get back to them as soon as we could. It took us until the next day to accept their offer. Details still needed to be worked out — denominational hoops needed to be jumped — but in our hearts Nancy and I knew we were soon going to be living in Valencia, and serving God through Glade Run.

The Big Vote

Part of the process in becoming the pastor of a church in the PCUSA at that time was to preach a candidating sermon in front of the prospective congregation. Following that, the members of the congregation voted whether to call you to be their pastor. While I was sure this was the church to which God was calling our family, the idea of one sermon being the determining factor in whether that would happen or not was rather intimidating. The sermon would be part of a regular morning worship service at Glade Run. The only part of the service I would lead would be the sermon itself. As the service started and we were singing the opening hymn my nose started bleeding. That was awkward. I put my hand to my nose and left the platform through the nearest door. The door led to the fellowship hall, where I searched for a tissue or paper towel. I eventually found paper towels in the church's kitchen. I tore off a portion of one and stuck it in the bleeding nostril. Blood soaked it in a few seconds. I replaced it with another, and another. In a couple of minutes the bleeding had nearly stopped. I stuffed a piece of paper towel into the nostril far enough that it wouldn't be visible and went back to the sanctuary. I wondered how I would sound with one stuffed nostril, but decided that would be better than the alternative of risking a bleeding nose while I preached. Finally, my moment came. As I looked out at the assembled congregation most seemed attentive. The members of the Pastor Nominating Committee were sitting in the front rows smiling and nodding encouragingly. It seemed to be a friendly audience.

Chapter 6

A Funny Thing Happened in the Kitchen

The Big Vote (Continued)

As it turns out it *was* a friendly audience. After the worship service, Nancy, Abby and I were escorted along with my Mom and Dad, who had come for the service, to a room in the church's office building where we would await the results of the vote. My mom asked, "What will you do if the vote is 51 percent to 49 percent?"

I said, "Oh, I'm not coming here unless the vote is 100 percent in favor."

I noticed two of the nominating committee's members, who had accompanied us to the office building, exchanging concerned looks. I had no way of knowing at the time, but these women had been part of Glade Run for a long time and neither of them remembered any congregational votes of importance being unanimous. Finally, the interim pastor came into the room with a somber look on his face. He was a gregarious type of guy so that gave me momentary pause. That was his intent. He brought a little slip of white paper containing the vote tally over to me. As he opened it, he smiled broadly and I saw the verdict: Yes-131, No-0. We were, indeed, coming to Glade Run.

When God's Timing Inhales

The vote took place in December of 1989, but with all the denominational formalities involved, we weren't scheduled to move to Valencia until Friday, February 2, 1990. My Mom and Dad had made arrangements to come out to help us with the move at the end of the week. Everything was looking up! We were coming *home,* where we would be serving in a church that was excited to have us on board. Abby would grow up with both sets of grandparents nearby and all was right with the world.

Except it wasn't.

On Tuesday, January 30, I was attending my final staff meeting at Crestview. The secretary interrupted the meeting to tell me I had a phone call from my Dad. I will never forget his words, "Your Mom had a stroke and it doesn't look good." I told Dad I would be home right away. Of course, right away would mean a minimum of six hours, because that's how long it would take to drive from Cincinnati to Gipsy. I went home to tell Nancy what was going on and that I had to leave right away. She said she and Abby would come with me. It wouldn't take long to get ready.

I was so upset that I said, "I don't have time. I have to go — now." As Nancy urged me to take a little extra time so she and Abby could get ready our phone rang. It was Dad.

"There's no need to rush. Your mother is gone," he said.

No. No. No. This couldn't be happening. Mom had waited years for this moment. We had been away from Pennsylvania for nine years. She had been longing for another granddaughter, and now we had Abby. This couldn't be happening. But it was. Friday, February 2, was supposed to be a wonderful day. Instead, I was presiding at Mom's funeral. We were all in shock. Instead of celebrating the move back home, we were talking about Mom's victory as she entered her eternal home with Jesus. But it didn't feel like a victory at that moment. Mom was only sixty-seven. She had so much more life ahead of her.

But now she didn't.

I was angry with God. I asked Him why He did this. Of course, He didn't *do* it. He permitted it—but God hadn't given my mother a stroke. He hadn't taken her life. He had welcomed her to be with Him, and as much as I tried to look at it that way I couldn't. Intellectually, I could say, "She's better off," and I knew it was true, but my heart was broken. Instead of heading into the new work at Glade Run filled with enthusiasm and joy, I limped to the starting gate. I was genuinely joyful about the opportunity to serve as Glade Run's pastor, but I was hurting more emotionally than anyone imagined. I couldn't think of how God's timing could have been any worse. Obviously, much worse things could've happened, but in the moment I couldn't picture them. The funny thing is even in that moment God *was* working. He gave me strength that I didn't possess to move forward. He helped me to see I was able to be there for my Dad, who needed me. It is true that in *all* things God works for the good of those who love Him and are called according to His purpose, but some of those things "inhale" at the time.

A Vision of the Church

As a senior pastor for the first time, I turned to God for a vision of His church, and particularly of a vision for Glade Run Church. Pastor Andy Weigand had told me many years before that when God calls a person into ministry He gives him or her a vision of the church. In a general way, that had been true when I was seventeen and heard God's call to become a pastor. My vision of the church then was as a center for bringing lost people to Jesus. As I served at Crestview the main vision God gave me was to call young people to faith in Jesus, and to lead adults into deeper relationships with Him.

As I prayed for God's vision of the church at Glade Run, the answer came through a passage of Scripture — Acts 2:42–47. The passage recounts life in the early church as the apostles established an order for their life together. The passage makes it clear the church is not a building but a gathering of people who have a common purpose — to know Jesus Christ as Savior and Lord, to share the truth about Him and to meet the needs of everyone. When people commit themselves to being the Church, God *shows up*, through signs and wonders and by adding people to the number of those being saved on a daily basis. That vision of the church motivated me through my time at Glade Run and continues to motivate me today.

If you are a follower of Jesus Christ, and you participate in a local church, ask yourself whether the Acts 2:42–47 vision of the church is what motivates and drives your local church. Are you seeking to grow in your understanding of Jesus' teaching? Are you devoted to prayer and fellowship? Are you meeting one another's needs? Is God intervening with miracles and adding people to your fellowship? While not many churches experience all of those realities in twenty-first century America, I continue to ask myself those questions, and continue to use this model as the standard, because God's desire for us to know Him through His Son, Jesus, and to make Him known is always at the center of our lives.

You Can't Always Have Your Dreams

A little more than a year after arriving at Glade Run, I was introduced to a ministry called *Logos*. The ministry was an approach for a whole church to focus on children and young people from kindergarten through twelfth grade based on Acts 2:42. I was impressed. In fact, after participating in a three-day training workshop intended to introduce and demonstrate the Logos ministry to churches and to equip them to implement it, which I attended with one of our volunteer leaders, Gloria Dillner, we returned eager to see Glade Run transformed into a local church that ministered to its children and young people in ways that I had never seen in a local church. It was early August and I believed God was going to see this ministry happen by the time school started in September.

I thought the best way to introduce this ministry and to get people on board was through my Sunday message that week. Part way through the message I said, "Look at the person sitting on your right. Now look at the person sitting on your left. Either you or one of the people you looked at a moment ago is going to be involved in the Logos ministry this fall! We need one third of us to take part in providing this vital ministry for our children and young people." I presented the vision passionately. I believed what I said was going to happen, but the idea that it could possibly happen so soon was absurd to some of the folks in the service that day.

As I greeted folks after worship, one of them walked up to me and said, "It's good to have dreams, but you can't always have your dreams." It was deflating. I thought about the statement for a moment and then said to myself: *This isn't a dream. This is a vision from God. This is going to happen.* Over the next several weeks, we assembled a Logos leadership team. We prayed for God to call people to the ministry. We started contacting folks and asking them to serve in one of the four areas of ministry in Logos based on Acts 2:42: worship, fellowship, study, and recreation. When the Logos ministry started in mid-September one out of every three adults who had heard my impassioned plea for their participation was, indeed, participating—including the woman who had told me you can't always have your dreams. It is true that you can't always have your dreams, but when God gives a vision, He often speaks that vision to others as well. When that happens, dreams and visions come true and amazing things can happen!

Once a Youth Pastor

As time passed, I realized something: I was now a senior pastor, but my heart was still in youth ministry. I had become the high school Bible teacher for the Logos ministry, and was involved with their recreation time as well. I also taught the high school Sunday school class rather than an adult class for my first couple of years at Glade Run. When I arrived, we had only a few young people in middle school and high school combined. After I'd been there for a few years, the high school group had grown to more than thirty people, and because of the Logos model of ministry more than half a dozen adults were directly involved in working with them. The funny thing was focusing on high school students, even tailoring the content of my messages to a ninth-grade reading level made the same messages accessible to everyone, including the adults.

The church was growing fairly rapidly. It was a lot of fun. The pain of Mom's death was still there, but all of the positive momentum in the church, particularly in the Logos ministry made it easy to focus on what was going right, what was being gained instead of what I had lost. That's another funny thing about life: We can't avoid pain and loss, but when we live into the blessings God provides in the midst of our pain and loss, our lives are truly blessed and we can be a blessing to others.

Leftovers

As Glade Run grew, so did the responsibilities of being the pastor. More people meant more visits when people went to the hospital or found themselves homebound. It meant more preparation for various ministries, and more meetings to organize and coordinate all that was happening. As my calendar filled with all of these good opportunities, a major challenge became obvious: I could not continue to do everything on my calendar and also invest the time necessary to be a good husband and dad. By this time Emmy had been born. With a wife and two daughters at home I found myself making difficult choices all of the time.

Decades later I heard Andy Stanley say pastors are going to cheat either the church or their families. His advice — cheat the church. That's good advice whether we're pastors or not, because it isn't only pastors who have to make the difficult choice of whether to invest more time at work or home. One afternoon, I had decided to make a pastoral call in the home of one of our elderly members before heading home for the day. I had told Nancy I would be home at 5 p.m. The visit started a little after 4 p.m. We sat down at the kitchen table. As I sat there, I noticed the kitchen stove in the background and a little clock hanging on the wall above it. The woman started telling me about her aches and pains. Then she told me about her family and how her children and grandchildren didn't come to visit her often. She continued by talking about the church and her thoughts about some of the ministries. I listened and nodded my head in agreement at various points. I kept glancing up at the clock every now and then, knowing I was supposed to be home by 5 p.m. This was long before the days of cell phones so I couldn't text Nancy to let her know I would be running a little late, but I was going to be late.

As the woman continued to talk 5 p.m. came and went; then 5:15. At 5:30 I noticed a pan sitting on the back of the stove. A thought came to my mind. I believe God spoke to me in it. Here's the thought: *If you put your family on the back burner long enough, they'll start to feel like leftovers.* I was already half an hour late. In that moment, I made a commitment that Nancy and the girls were not going to feel like leftovers, or if they did, they weren't going to feel that way anymore. I interrupted the woman, asked her if I could pray with her, and then excused myself to go home. From that day to this, I've made a concerted effort never to make my family feel like leftovers.

Challenging the Status Quo

The longer I served at Glade Run, the more I realized everything was going to be a challenge when it came to moving forward

131

regardless of the ministry area. Glade Run was a long established church. While I had been told in the interview process that the three primary goals for the new pastor were to revitalize worship, bring children and young people back to the church, and renew the church's long-held focus on mission, each time we proposed something that would address one of those key areas, we experienced push back. The push back might come in the form of one or more of the longstanding members being upset. It might come in the form of the cherished seven last words of the church, "We've never done it that way before." It might come in the form of a lack of volunteers to carry out the new direction. Over time, though, when we challenged the status quo, it changed. The Logos ministry addressed the desire for children and young people to come back into the church. While the transition was never easy or smooth, the joy of having children and young people integrally involved in the life and worship of the church was a blessing that all could affirm, or nearly all.

The transition in worship came more slowly and will be addressed later, but it was the most difficult change to address. The key challenge was always what constituted vital worship. The renewal on the long-held mission focus of the church came more easily, because the changes didn't impact as many folks directly. As first the young people, and then the adults started participating in short-term mission projects, the culture of the congregation started changing. People started seeing the importance of not only praying for missionaries and sending money to support them and their mission causes, but also going ourselves. God spoke to folks who participated in the trips, and it became obvious that the new status quo was that in addition to people giving their treasures (their money), they would give their time and talents as well by going into the world to share Jesus' good news.

Experiencing God

With renewed life and vitality being poured into the congregation by the children and young people's participation in worship and various activities of the church, and with the renewed emphasis on mission, a number of adults started asking me to provide a study about what it meant to grow in their faith and commitment to Jesus. As I prayed about what to study, one of Nancy's cousins told me about a book she had been reading and an accompanying workbook. It was titled *Experiencing God*. The author was Henry Blackaby.

As I read through the book, it became clear this was precisely the study we needed. One of the most helpful aspects of the book was Blackaby's assumption that God is always working among us and inviting us to participate in that work. He also told his readers *how* God communicates with us. His common sense explanation was clear and compelling. Blackaby tells us God speaks to us in four primary ways: 1) through the Bible (God's written word); 2) through prayer; 3) through our circumstances; and 4) through other believers.

Blackaby pointed out that the level of certainty we have about whether it is actually God speaking to us diminishes as we move from one means to the next.

We always know God is speaking to us when we read the Bible because it is God-inspired material.

When we pray, the Holy Spirit speaks to us, but sometimes we might also speak to ourselves and convince ourselves it is God. This is particularly true when we want something a great deal, and want to convince ourselves that God is going to give it.

Sometimes our circumstances might be God speaking to us, such as when we pray for God to open a door to a certain type of ministry, such as men's ministry, and then a recovery center for men working through addictions opens in our area, and we have the opportunity to get involved with them. At other times, though, circumstances might not be God speaking at all. We must exercise care when determining when God is speaking through our circumstances.

Finally, when other believers tell us God has spoken to them on our behalf, they might be speaking the truth. It might also be a means used by others in attempts to convince us their opinion is God's will. Folks have used that approach on me on a fairly regular basis over the years in my work as a pastor. Folks come and say, "Pastor Chris, God told me _____." The blank is usually filled with some change the person wants the church to make because the current practice isn't personally fulfilling, or is even personally offensive to him or her.

While I have experienced God's word to me through others many times over the years, especially through folks such as Nancy, Andy Weigand, and Mert Bomgaars, Blackaby makes it clear we must be certain God has actually spoken before we accept the advice of others and move forward. Working through *Experiencing God* proved quite helpful for the participants in understanding both how God is at work around us, and how we might participate in that work. If you are interested in hearing God's voice in your life, and in discerning and doing His will, I recommend *Experiencing God* as a book to help you with that kind of discernment.

A Vision of the Lost

Ever since I trusted Jesus as my Savior and Lord at the age of twelve, I've had a burden for the lost—for those who haven't yet trusted Jesus as their Savior and Lord. Jesus made it clear we are called to go out and look for the lost and to invite them to join us in God's family. He once said it isn't the will of our Father in Heaven that even one of these little ones should perish.

As Glade Run became more involved in short-term mission work, so did I. I started to participate in trips to Kentucky and Mexico on a regular basis, making at least one trip each year, and often two trips. As I prepared for one particular trip, a trip to Kentucky, I was in my family room praying. As I prayed, I had a vision—yes, a vision. I've had two visions in my life, and both of them occurred during my time at Glade Run. (Maybe I had both of my visions while I was at Glade Run because, as the prophet Joel tells us, young men will have visions, and old men will dream dreams.) In this first vision, I was praying and was fully awake, yet I saw a rural area in front of me. I sat at the edge of a great chasm, and as I looked over the edge thousands and thousands of people were trying to climb out. The walls were too steep to climb so many of the people were trampling one another. Their faces wore expressions of desperation. The atmosphere around them was dark and thick. The vision lasted only a short time, perhaps five minutes. The vision was quite vivid. Its meaning seemed clear—these folks would be lost if they didn't get out of the chasm. Their number seemed to represent all of the lost people of the world, and yet they also represented a specific group of lost people: those in rural areas. I'm not certain whether the rural area in the vision was in the United States, another nation, or whether it represented any rural area. It might simply have represented the desolation of lost people living without Jesus.

I've reflected on that vision countless times over the years, and it has heightened my passion for reaching lost people, particularly those in rural areas near and far. While my description of the vision might seem strange to you, or might confirm an experience you've had in your own life, I'm sure the vision came from God. First, the vision's focus was the need of the lost for a Savior. Why would anyone but God care about giving me such a picture? You might think it was my imagination, because I was praying in preparation for a mission trip, but I wasn't thinking of lost people in the moment the vision came. I wasn't tired so it wasn't a dream, and, as I mentioned I was fully awake. As I reflected on the vision in order to write these words the images came back to me. I am even surer God wanted to impress on my heart His concern for the lost, and my call to be an advocate for them. Visions must certainly be listed as one of those funny things God has used throughout history to get our attention and to anchor His call in our hearts.

No Need to Pray

As Glade Run kept growing—particularly as the children and youth ministry, and worship attendance kept growing—it became clear that in order to continue to minister to more people we needed to add an addition to the facilities. I've often heard my friend John Nuzzo, the pastor of Victory Family Church, a vibrant growing church in Cranberry Township, Pennsylvania say, "I have never prayed about whether to build more buildings. When God sends more people, and we run out of space, we add on to accommodate them." That makes sense, doesn't it? Sometimes God speaks through our circumstances. An increasing number of people coming to Jesus in our church is a circumstance God uses to tell us it is time to build.

Because Glade Run was a Presbyterian Church, we approached the growth in a decent and orderly manner. We put together a building team to consider our options. We contracted with an architect to listen to our needs and to put together a proposal. When the architect came back to meet with us after our initial meeting, he showed us some preliminary drawings that made it clear he had not listened to our needs. His proposed addition was in the location we said we did not want to build it. It included a dramatic change to the front of the existing building, which had been in the community for nearly a hundred years. The cost of the proposal was prohibitive. The presentation cast a discouraged pall over the team. I could see while we might not need to pray over whether to build a building, it would take a great deal of prayer to move us forward after this discouraging setback.

Do You Know What You Need?

Through my experience with Logos, I had become friends with Dr. Dale Milligan, the organization's founder. I went to visit him after our building team had met with the architect. I expressed my disappointment and anger over the direction the meeting had gone. Dale listened for a while and then asked a simple question, "Do you know what you need?"

"Of course, I do," I responded. I explained we needed a gym where the young people could play and the recreational aspect of the Logos program could be experienced through the winter months when outdoor activities weren't possible. I told him we needed a vastly expanded fellowship hall where we could experience the family dinnertime with our growing number of children and young people. In addition, we needed a youth room and some additional classrooms for our preschool.

"Could you draw what you need on graph paper?" Dale asked. Sure. Nancy and I had experience in drawing floor plans from her management and equipment class in college, and my carpentry experience had given me the ability to envision what the drawings would become. I left the meeting excited and determined to draw what we needed so the building team could see it was not only possible for us to expand, but practical, as well. Nancy was eager for the opportunity. That night after we had put the girls to bed, we worked on the floor plan until well after midnight. When we finished I was sure the drawing before us was exactly what we needed. We had repurposed some of the existing building space and had drawn what the architect would later call a "background building," that while much larger than the architect's original proposal didn't detract from the original beauty of the nearly one-hundred-year-old church building at the front of the property. It would also cost much less to build.

We called another meeting of the building team and when I showed them the proposed building, one of the members asked, "Why didn't you show us this before?"

"I thought we were supposed to come up with the ideas together," I said. "I didn't know the architect wasn't going to listen to us." It was one of those times when I knew God wanted something to be accomplished, and He had given Nancy and me the skills and abilities to make that something clear to others. The building team agreed. I contended we needed to get an architect and move forward with the plans. The rest of the team reminded me that we had an architect. I couldn't understand why we would want to use him when he had so clearly not listened to what we said in the first place, but the team was convinced he would be the most economical choice.

We arranged for another meeting, and when the architect saw the graph paper drawings, he raised some questions. He wasn't sure the department of labor and industry would approve several aspects of the building. He told us it was a "background building" that would never win any architectural awards. No. It would not and has not, but it would provide much more practically useable space than his original proposal and at a far lower cost. The congregation voted to move forward with the revised project. We put together a financial campaign to provide the funds to see it become a reality, and the process moved forward quite smoothly.

A Vision of the Tombstone

The plans were finalized and sent out for bid. A team from the board of trustees worked with a local bank to obtain financing. Contractors were lined up to do the work, and work was scheduled to begin. The week before the actual construction process began, I had another vision. While the first vision was easy to understand this one was not. As I prayed, again while fully awake, I saw a giant tombstone in the back parking lot of the church. It was in the location where the new fellowship hall would be constructed. The tombstone was taller than the existing building. No words were inscribed on it, but it was definitely an old-fashioned tombstone, as you would see in a Civil War era cemetery. The vision lasted for a couple of minutes. When it ended I wondered what it meant. I asked God what it meant. Nothing. I prayed and reflected and reflected and prayed. Nothing. I asked myself: *What are the possible meanings of the vision?*

I had no doubt it was a vision. It was as vivid as the vision of the chasm. As I thought and prayed it occurred to me that it could mean the project was dead. It also occurred to me that it could mean, unless we continued to remember the true church is the people within the building and not the building, the building addition would be of no more value than a tombstone, which simply marks the location of a dead person.

I received no clarity regarding the vision's meaning, whether either or neither of my interpretations was right. Then another thought hit me, "Should I tell the congregation about the vision?" It didn't seem like the kind of vision to share with the entire church family at the outset of construction, especially when I had no idea what it meant. The more I thought about it, the more certain I became the people needed to know. I shared the vision, but prefaced it by saying in the time of the prophet Samuel of Israel, God made certain none of Samuel's words "fell to the ground," in other words every statement Samuel made came from God, and carried out an effective purpose. I told the folks I had experienced a vision that week and did not know what it meant. I told them the timing of the vision and of sharing it seemed bad because we were going into a major building project. Then I shared the vision, and offered the two possible interpretations that had come to me. I told the folks that either of the two interpretations could be true, but that neither of them needed to be true so long as we continued to put Jesus first, and continued to remember we and not a building are the church.

While several hundred people heard my comments only one person came to me afterward to say anything. He said, "I think it was stupid to share a vision like that right when we're getting ready to build such a big addition." I couldn't disagree. As it turned out, the building progressed on schedule and on budget. When it opened it was a great blessing to the church family and to the surrounding community. While I no longer serve Glade Run, the building is still being used effectively. Whatever the vision meant, it did not mark the end of God's work there.

The Explosion

As we prepared to open the new building, a number of folks on the worship team paid a visit to Ginghamsburg United Methodist Church outside of Dayton, Ohio. Ginghamsburg had been a small, rural church, much like Glade Run when a pastor named Mike Slaughter went there to serve. He introduced a new style of worship and many other changes, and the church exploded with growth. By the time of our visit, Ginghamsburg had become a large church family serving thousands of people. They had impressive facilities and a "contemporary" style of worship. (I put the word "contemporary" in quotes, because as Pastor Rick Warren has aptly noted, "All worship music is contemporary. The only question is contemporary to which century?") We were impressed. We had been considering revamping the worship services at Glade Run, and had started experimenting with blended worship, which meant we had used some traditional elements in the service along with some contemporary elements. The experiment had met with mixed reviews.

Some of the folks loved the changes, while others hated them. That kind of response typically doesn't end well.

I soon made sure it didn't end well.

It was not my intention to cause an explosion, at least not of the negative kind, after our visit to Ginghamsburg, but I decided we needed to make a radical adjustment to our worship experiment. We needed to move to a fully, contemporary style worship service. This was in a church that had been as traditional as any church in western Pennsylvania when I had visited there a half dozen years earlier. Our modest adjustments to the services hadn't prepared the congregation for the drastic changes they would experience when they arrived the following weekend. Like Ginghamsburg, we had an explosion. Unlike Ginghamsburg, it wasn't an explosion of growth. The change effectively divided the church family. Some loved it; others hated it. There was little middle ground. Thankfully, with the construction of the new building nearly complete, we had a workable solution: We would use the new gym as a worship space for a contemporary service, and the sanctuary as the worship space for a traditional service. Rather than blend worship styles or choose one over the other, we moved to two, distinct worship gatherings in two distinct locations in the building.

When folks ask me about that era of my life, I always say it was as close to Hell as I ever want to come. My goal was never to upset so many people, but my eagerness to reach lost people overcame my common sense. Had I thought or prayed about it more, I would undoubtedly have come to the realization that such drastic changes needed to be introduced more incrementally. They would likely have been received more willingly had we developed a "bless and add" approach. By that I mean we would have blessed what we were already doing with the traditional worship service, and added a contemporary service. That's what we did in the end, but the abrupt process of radical change on the front end was a shock to many. It was perhaps the single least effective decision I've ever made as a pastor and leader. A bit more prayer and patience would have been extremely helpful. It was a time when listening for God's voice was needed, but I hadn't started there. The funny thing is God worked through the situation despite my impatience and lack of wisdom and common sense. Over time, the church grew rapidly once again.

Speak to Me God!

During that time of discontent, which was primarily of my own making, I came to a particularly low moment. I had started to participate in a three-year leadership-training program offered by Asbury Seminary known as The Beeson Institute for Advanced Church Leadership. Every three months participants traveled either to Asbury Seminary or to a church somewhere in the United States to experience firsthand the aspect of the leadership training that particular module of the institute emphasized. (It was at one of those onsite events at Ginghamsburg United Methodist Church that I had been introduced to reaching the lost through contemporary worship.) Another module "happened" to be scheduled for the week after a particularly difficult weekend at Glade Run. I was extremely discouraged. As I drove out of the church parking lot that afternoon on my way to experience the module titled Visionary Leadership, I felt nothing like a visionary or a leader. In fact, as I drove out of the parking lot I had one of my frank conversations with God. I said, "God, I'm not coming back here unless you make me. In fact, I'm not going to eat again until you tell me exactly what I'm supposed to do next."

I'd never been quite that direct with God in asking, or more accurately, demanding He tell me what I was supposed to do next. As I drove to Asbury Seminary, which is where the module on visionary leadership was being held, I reflected on everything taking place at the time. To be more accurate, I complained to God about everything that wasn't going the way I thought it was supposed to go. I complained about the sacrifices I had made in order to serve Him. I wanted to show God that He owed me an answer. Every so often I stopped to listen. Nothing. Each time was the same. Tell God why He had to answer me because of all I was doing for Him. Stop to listen. Nothing. The drive from Valencia to Asbury took nearly seven hours. That's a lot of time to present one's case to God, or at least it seemed that way to me. I checked into my room and was getting hungry. I hadn't eaten since breakfast. I would be getting a lot hungrier over the next few days.

I turned in early that night so I woke up early on Monday morning. I sat there in the room listening. I decided if I expected God to speak to me, the least I could do was listen. I sat there for a long time. Thoughts flooded my head as I waited. God would surely answer, wouldn't He? How long was it going to take? My mind focused on the situation back home. When were we going to move through the disagreements and get back to the business of reaching lost people again? My mind turned to the agenda for the week: Visionary Leadership. I still wasn't feeling much like a visionary or a leader. Then the questions started popping into my mind: Should I even be a pastor? Was this all worth it? Wouldn't it be easier to use my talents in the business world? I tried to keep such thoughts out of my mind, because I wanted to hear God's answer when He spoke, but it was a constant battle to keep focused on listening for His voice in the midst of so much chatter. Eventually, I had to get ready for the day's conference.

No answer. No breakfast.

During the day, I met another pastor from Pennsylvania named Dave. We hit it off and before long I was telling him about my commitment not to eat until God had spoken to me. He looked at me incredulously. His expression made it clear he wanted to say something like, "Really? You expect God to speak to you and tell you clearly what He wants you to do next?" He didn't say a word, nor did he need to. His expression said it all. We went through the day's lectures. The information was helpful, but no word from God was in them. No direct word from God came either. Dave asked me if I wanted to go to dinner. I said I would be glad to join him, but wouldn't be eating, because I hadn't heard from God. We were both glad for the company. Dave told me about his church, family, and his plans for the future. As he finished up and we walked out the restaurant door, I said, "All I want is for God to give me some kind of a sign."

At that very moment a large bird flew overhead and deposited a "sign" on my head. I reached up and felt it. There was a lot. Dave looked at me. We both roared with laughter. I returned to my serious mode and said, "I don't know if that's a sign from God, but if it is I don't get it." I went back to the room and listened again. Nothing. I reviewed the day's notes. Nothing. I decided to turn in early again.

I woke up famished on Tuesday morning, and my head was pounding, most likely from a lack of caffeine. I returned to my listening, and being interrupted by my thoughts and questions, but still nothing from God. I got ready for the day's lectures. John Maxwell was scheduled to speak, and I knew he would be both interesting and helpful. What I didn't know was he would be the one to start the breakthrough I'd been asking God to give me.

To be honest, I don't remember anything John said that day. I do remember after he finished for the day, a number of folks stood in line to speak with him. I was the last one in line. When my turn came I told John quickly of my struggles and of my desperation for God to show me the next step. I told him I was ready to give up. I don't remember his specific words to me. I do remember he said, "Sit down." He and I sat down on the steps at the front of the lecture room. He challenged and encouraged me to persevere through the difficulties I was facing because God was going to use me. Then he put his hand on my head and prayed for me.

It was one of the most important moments in my life.

I had heard John Maxwell speak before. I knew he often left immediately after speaking to travel to another place, but because he was scheduled to speak again the next day he had stayed later that day. In my limited experience, I had not seen him invest the kind of time he gave me to listen, lend a word of advice, and pray with someone at any other event. It was a holy moment for me. I still didn't know what God was going to do or say, but I knew He was calling me to continue in my work at Glade Run. God had definitely spoken through another person—John Maxwell—in that moment.

Breakthrough

I went back to my room and decided to listen again. After a time, God spoke. He said, "Go back and apologize to the people of Glade Run because you haven't been giving everything you have to serve them in my name. Tell them your joy is not going to be dependent on what they do, but on Me. Tell them you will be with them for five more years." I didn't write the instructions down at the time—but they were clear as a bell. As Dr. Willis would have said, they were written on the "hatband of my heart." I felt them as much as heard them. I would go back to these words many times in the days ahead, after returning to Glade Run, because the work didn't get easier simply because God had assured me I was called to continue serving there. As you will also see, the third instruction would ultimately be the only one I was unable to fulfill. God would give me further instructions there.

When I returned home and told the folks at the worship services the next weekend what God had said, not too many of them responded. One particular man, who was an elder, came up to me afterwards and said, "I forgive you, and I will be back to serve with you." He had taken a leave of absence from serving on the Session (the board of elders) for a period of time. I hadn't known why. My commitment to put God absolutely first, and to serve Him more faithfully in Jesus' name in the power of the Holy Spirit, was enough for the man to return to serving.

Several months after my comments, another person who served on the church staff came to me and said, "I was skeptical when you said you were going to get your joy from God and not from how the people responded to your leadership, but I see a big difference in you. I want you to tell me how to do that, too. How do you get your joy from God no matter what people do?" Those two affirmations made it clear God had, indeed, spoken to me. As God had responded to Gideon's fleece, God had responded to me. That's a truly funny thing: the God of the universe responds to the challenges of those

He has created to show Himself or to speak to us. He hasn't always done it, and He is under no obligation to do it, but it meant the world to me that He did it at that moment, because I needed it so desperately. That has been one of the defining moments not only in my ministry, but also in my relationship with God.

The Second Explosion

We worked our way through the worship challenges, moved into the new building, and saw participation in all of our ministries and worship continue to grow. People came to trust Jesus as their Savior and Lord for the first time and it seemed life was settling in once again in an ongoing, positive direction. As we turned the calendar to the year 2000 — Y2K — it seemed I would be at Glade Run, not only for the five more years God had directed me to stay back in 1997, but for many years to come. The only potential challenge to that future was the denomination's move away from traditional biblical truth. I had survived my years in seminary by digging deeper into the Bible and fellowshipping with others who held firmly to the truths we found there. Having first Arthur Pace and then Pastor Gary Pemberton as supervising pastors, both men of deep faith and conviction, I had been more deeply grounded in biblical faith. The Presbyterian Church USA had always held beliefs with which I disagreed, but as I had said when I pursued ordination, one has only two choices when he or she finds the teachings and direction of the church or denomination incorrect: 1) leave and find a more faithful one; or 2) stay and fight to bring it back to faithfulness. That fight had been going on for sixteen years and I saw few, if any, signs that the denomination — meaning the PCUSA — was moving back toward faithfulness.

The PCUSA's stance on abortion had been pro-abortion in certain situations. It had written a position paper in the 1970s stating abortion could be an act of faithful stewardship in certain circumstances. I had never agreed with that. At the denomination's annual meeting in the summer of 2000 a position paper had been received that said Jesus Christ might not be the only way to salvation. I definitely could not agree with that. The denomination had made a commitment to add a section to the *Book of Order* — its declaration of the way the church, its leaders, and members are to live — to prohibit pastors from performing same-sex unions. I saw this as a step toward faithfulness. Then in January of 2001, a friend who served as the pastor of another PCUSA church called and asked me to go to lunch with him. After some pleasantries he asked me what I was going to do when the amendment to the *Book of Order* regarding same-sex unions failed. I said, "If that happens, I'm done." He attempted to show me I needed to stay and fight. His most compelling argument was in five years from that time, the denomination would split over the matter and we would be able to leave and keep our buildings and church funds.

I asked Him, "And what do I say to Jesus if He comes back in two?" In other words, if Jesus kept His promise of returning to the earth to establish His eternal reign in two years, what would I say to Him? Would I say the buildings and funds were more important to me than being faithful to promoting His truth in love? This was an extremely difficult moment. I was in the fourth year of that five-year period of time God had initiated in 1997. I loved the people of Glade Run and the entire ministry God was doing through us. I didn't want to leave this local body of believers who had become my family through everything we had experienced together.

I also knew this denominational decision would be an extremely divisive matter for us. While nearly everyone at Glade Run would have taken the same conservative, biblical view of the matters mentioned above as I, many were extremely loyal to the denomination, and to the idea of bringing the church back to faithfulness. While I had become a part of the PCUSA as an adult, many of them and their families had been in the denomination and its antecedent denominations for generations.

When Nancy and I talked and prayed about the matter, it was clear we couldn't continue in the PCUSA if my friend were right. We started to consider what would happen if I were no longer at Glade Run. My first thought was to do carpentry work to pay the bills and then possibly to start a church in Cranberry Township, a rapidly growing area immediately to the west of us. We considered leaving the area because our goal would never be to divide Glade Run, a church family we had come to love deeply. We sought only to be faithful to our own understanding of God's truth in the Bible. The plan of action became to wait and see what happened with the vote on the amendment. Perhaps my friend was wrong about the outcome. We would respond according to the outcome of the actual vote. We held meetings at Glade Run to discuss the denomination's impending vote, and during them I told the people I could no longer serve the PCUSA if the amendment failed.

When Push Comes to Shove

In March the amendment failed. I drove to the Presbytery office in Zelienople to renounce the jurisdiction of the PCUSA. That meant I would no longer be recognized as a pastor in that denomination. I had hoped for a transition period of at least several weeks or months, but in that meeting it became clear the Presbytery would be following the *Book of Order* protocol to the letter. They would send an administrative commission, a group of outside elders and pastors, to oversee Glade Run for whatever period of time I remained there. After having served for more than eleven years as the pastor of Glade Run, I knew the people of Glade Run would not be served well for any period of time in such a situation. If I ever wanted God to speak to me verbally, it was at that moment. He did not. The events of the next few days would make it clear He was working actively and powerfully in our lives.

That evening several men helped me move my books, files and the accumulated effects of more than a decade of ministry out of my study at Glade Run. We stacked everything in our garage. Afterward they stood with me in a small circle in our driveway. We joined hands and prayed. It was a powerful reminder to me that God's church is always people, not buildings, not positions, not titles. As Jesus said, "Wherever two or more are gathered in my name, I am there with you."

Finished and Free

As I had driven home from the Presbytery office that Tuesday afternoon two competing sequences of thought had come to mind. First, I thought, *I'm nobody. I'm no longer a pastor. I no longer have a church to serve. I have no idea what's going to happen to my family and me.* No sooner had those thoughts flashed through my mind than the second series came and competed for attention, *I'm free! I can now do exactly what God calls me to do, whatever it is. I can follow the Bible as the only* Book of Order *for my life.* Those thoughts battled for supremacy as I drove home. One moment I would be despondent because I was no longer a pastor. In the next I would be nearly euphoric because I knew God had to show up now. I had put Him first in this situation, and He promises when we put Him first He will care for our needs. I was finished and free. I had no idea how quickly God would show up, but He was about to open a door I would never have expected.

The news of my departure from Glade Run spread quickly. Nancy and I started receiving phone calls and emails asking, "What are we going to do?" We explained I was going to go to work as a carpenter. We weren't sure what the next step would be. Many folks said, "You helped us come to know Jesus," and then asked, "Are you going to abandon us?"

I hadn't considered that. Nancy and I were being faithful to Jesus when we left the PCUSA. We knew if we stayed in the area long-term people might decide to become part of the new church. We didn't want to hurt the people of Glade Run. But maybe we weren't supposed to leave the area, after all. We wouldn't be deciding for other people by staying in western Pennsylvania. As it turned out, many of them had already decided as we had. The denomination's decision was the last straw for them, too. Many folks who called us that week asked whether we could have a prayer meeting on Sunday simply to get together and pray for God's direction. We agreed and said we would find a place.

On Thursday morning, one of the families who had decided not to continue in the PCUSA had a daughter who was having surgery. I drove to Pittsburgh to be with them before the surgery. As I walked into the hospital room, Amy, the mother asked, "Chris, what are you doing here? You don't have to be here."

"I don't *have* to do anything," I said. "I'm here because I love you all and we need to pray for Shanna." After we prayed and waited together, I headed home. On the way, I decided to stop and see a businessman, named Mark, who owned a larger house that would accommodate Sunday evening's prayer meeting, to see whether we could meet there. When I stopped and asked him, he said we would be welcome on any other night, but Sunday night was his younger son's birthday party. I thanked him and started to leave.

He asked, "By the way, what's the plan?"

"What plan?" I asked.

"The plan. What are you going to do?" He asked.

I said, "I'm going to do carpentry work to pay the family's bills for a while. Then eventually I'm going to start a church in Cranberry."

"Is that the only plan?" He asked.

"If I could support my family, I would start the church now," I replied.

He said, "That's what I was hoping you would say." He went over to his cash drawer and pulled out an envelope that had my name on it. He said he had been trying to figure out how to get it to me. Then he said, "Let's get started." He handed me the envelope, and prayed for me.

I walked out envelope in hand, got in my car, drove up the road a short distance, and pulled over to see what was in it. The envelope contained $2,000. I drove home and showed the money to Nancy and the girls. We sat together and prayed about whether God was using it to tell us to start a church. We agreed it was. Anybody will tell you that you couldn't start a church in America in 2001 with $2,000, but we believed it was God telling us we could. That was only the beginning.

The next day the phone rang and it was a young man, named David, who had been attending Glade Run for a while. He said, "Pastor Chris, I heard you're not at Glade Run anymore."

"That's right," I said.

"Could you use a church?" He asked.

I said, "You mean a church building?"

"Yes," he said. "My grandfather has a church building that he built and it's been empty for two years. I bet he would let you use it to start a church if you asked him."

I asked, "Where is this building?"

"Ivywood," he answered.

"Where's Ivywood?" I asked. We had been living in the area for eleven years, and we lived about six miles from Ivywood, but I had never been there. As I was about to find out, Ivywood is one of those places you find only if you're looking. After a little more discussion, we agreed I would stop over to see the building the next morning. It would be a day that changed everything.

On Saturday, March 31, 2001, I walked into the building of the Bible Baptist Church of Ivywood. Earl McRoberts, David's grandfather, soon joined us. He came walking into the building, supported by a cane as he walked. I'll never forget his first words, "Young man, I've been praying for God to send someone to fill this place up again. And I told Him, 'You're going to have to send him to me because I can't even go looking for him.'" I still get chills every time I remember that moment.

With tears in my eyes, I said, "Mr. McRoberts, I think I may be your man." We talked about the building, and the "terms" of using it, which were quite reasonable. All Mr. McRoberts asked was we pay the four missionaries that the church was still supporting at the rate of $25 per month, and pay the utilities. Under those conditions we could use the building as long as we wanted. We shook hands and that was that.

The next night we had our prayer meeting. I recounted the events of the previous week, as I have recounted them with you. When I got to the part about having a building where we could start our church, people cheered, and cried and praised God. New Life Christian Ministries had begun.

Chapter 7

A Funny Thing Happened in a Storm Door

The Amazing Beginning

About sixty people attended that original prayer meeting. I told them we would meet the following Tuesday evening to clean up the building, which had stood empty for more than two years. On Tuesday evening more than eighty people showed up for the cleanup night. While many were from Glade Run, some were also from the former Bible Baptist Church of Ivywood. When we had all gathered, and before the clean up began, we sat together in the worship center and thanked God for providing us a place to worship Him, to serve Him, and to tell others about the amazing truth and love of Jesus. We sang and prayed together. I thanked everyone for coming, and set forth the mission of New Life for the first time: we were going to share the new life of Jesus Christ with the world—one person at a time. It was an incredible moment for us to see how quickly God had provided so much for our new church family. That was only the beginning of what God would supply for our first official worship time together that upcoming Sunday.

As we cleaned the building, David came over to me and said, "Pastor Chris, what are we going to do about PowerPoint on Sunday?"

"PowerPoint?" I asked. "We aren't going to be able to have PowerPoint. I hope to get an overhead projector to show the words for the songs."

He said, "Well, we have some money, and I'm sure if you could get a projector and screen by Sunday we could pay for it."

"Who are we?" I asked.

"The church. We don't have any people, but we have some money." David told me that although the church had stopped meeting a couple of years before for various reasons, the checking account still had some funds, which had been used to pay for the missionaries and utilities over that time. He was sure because the projector and screen would be fixtures of the church building, it would be fine to use some of the funds for them. He would need to clear it with his grandfather who served as the trustee of the account.

After that David told me that back in 1957, when the building was built they had put a conduit under the floor of the worship center in case anything ever needed to be run from the front of the church to the back. It so happened we could run the computer cable through it so we could use a computer to operate the projector for the PowerPoint presentations from the back of the church. Now that's a funny thing, wouldn't you say? I was born in 1957, and in that very year a church building was constructed that would become the location of a newly formed church that I would pastor in 2001 — forty-four years later. Not only that, but conduit was put under the floor to provide for the use of technology that didn't even exist when it was placed there. That is an amazing coincidence. We *were* going to have PowerPoint for our first worship service after all.

Shortly after that conversation, a couple who led the worship team for the contemporary worship service at Glade Run, who had also come for clean up night, walked up to me and asked, "Who's leading worship on Sunday?"

"I don't know," I said. To be honest, I hadn't given it much thought, not being a detail person. They asked what time our worship service was going to be held. When I told them 10 a.m., they said they could lead worship at New Life and still fulfill their responsibilities at Glade Run's contemporary service. Just like that, we had both PowerPoint and a worship team for our first worship service. It's amazing what happens when ordinary people team up to serve our extraordinary God.

On Sunday, April 8, 2001, we celebrated our first worship service together. More than a hundred people came. We were in the middle of nowhere and more than a hundred people came, some of whom I didn't even know. It was nothing like I had imagined when I thought of doing carpentry work for a couple of years and then starting a church in Cranberry. It happened so quickly, and we were all so amazed at what God had provided in a matter of two weeks.

Even with the isolated location, we needed to add a second worship service by June, because we had already outgrown the small worship center. We were parking cars in a field behind the church because the Ivywood property was only seven-tenths of an acre. We started looking for property where we could build a bigger mission outpost to accommodate all of the people we believed God was going to bring to us. Even so, we saw God fulfilling our mission of "sharing the new life of Jesus Christ with the world—one person at a time." The emphasis is on *one* at a time. God always works in each of our lives that way — one at a time.

Transformation comes one person at a time. We have seen that time and time again through the years. In fact, if not for Mark's gift of $2,000, or David's phone call, or Mr. McRobert's generosity, New Life might never have started. Some would say, "Maybe it would have started a few years later in Cranberry and been much bigger because of the greater people base." Even if that had happened, we would still have had the opportunity to reach people one at a time. That's the amazing thing about God — Jesus died for *all* of us on the cross of Calvary, but He also died for each one of us, for you and for me. New Life's amazing beginning happened the same way all amazing beginnings do — one ordinary person offered the extraordinary truth and love of Jesus to another, then another.

If God Wants Us to Go

In the midst of New Life's amazing takeoff, we prepared to go on our first international mission trip that October. Because our mission included sharing the new life of Jesus with the "world," we wanted to root our ministry, not only in supporting missions and missionaries near and far, but also in sending teams to work with the missions and missionaries we supported right from the beginning. I was particularly enthusiastic about this trip because Emmy, who was not quite eight at the time, was going on her first mission trip to Mexico with me and she was eager. God had given her a heart for the people of Mexico. She had a children's book for learning Spanish, which she studied every day and she was fully engaged in the preparations. She packed her suitcase for the trip months before our scheduled departure date. More than thirty people signed up for the trip, and for a newly formed church family, this was going to be a big deal.

Remember the trip was scheduled to take place in October. It was 2001. On September 11, 2001, the United States experienced the tragic events of the destruction of the World Trade Center, the attack on the Pentagon, and the crash of flight 93 in Pennsylvania. That happened a little more than a month before the Mexico trip was to take place. That day changed everything. In the aftermath many people feared air travel. Travel in and out of the United States became more difficult, as the borders were guarded much more closely. Some members of the Mexico team questioned whether we ought to make the trip so soon after these tragic events. A meeting was called to pray, discuss the pros and cons, and decide whether to go. While the adults discussed and debated whether we ought to make the trip, Emmy lay on the floor coloring. At a certain point, Kathy, one of the trip's organizers said, "Emmy, what do you think?"

Emmy looked up from her coloring book. "I think if God wants us to go on the trip, He will keep us safe," she said. It was the simple, faithful response of a child. Emmy put her head back down and continued coloring. Emmy's brief response proved to be a turning point in the discussion. The group sat in silence for a moment, all eyes on Emmy. Then the majority decided she was right. They would go and trust God to protect us. Henry Blackaby reminds us that sometimes God speaks through other people. There's no doubt God spoke through Emmy that night.

That commitment started an uninterrupted string of annual mission trips in the United States and abroad to places such as Mexico, Jamaica, Alaska, Cambodia, West Virginia, China, North Carolina, Cuba, and New Orleans that continues to the current time. Those trips lend credence to our mission statement, which calls us to share the new life of Jesus Christ with the world. Such trips have reminded us we exist to reach folks who haven't yet been reached with the new life of Jesus. I've always wondered what would have happened to New Life's mission movement if Emmy hadn't made her simple, faith-filled comment back in September of 2001. One person often brings courage to many, and sometimes the person turns out to be someone we would least expect.

Let's Move

By early 2003, we had outgrown the Ivywood property. Our commitment to be an "indigenous" church from the beginning, meaning we would approach worship and ministry by using the language, dress, music, and technology of the local people, as a missionary going to a foreign country would learn and use the indigenous people's language and culture as the starting point for sharing the Good News of Jesus, attracted many people who either didn't go to church, or who had given up on church as typically presented. We had been looking, without success, for another piece of property nearby where we could build a facility that would accommodate our growing church family, and give us the ability to continue to share the new life of Jesus with more and more people in our community and region. We had even investigated the possibility of buying 200 acres of land immediately behind the Ivywood property, but nothing worked out at the time.

Jim Brown, one of our elders, suggested we look into moving to the local high school. It had an auditorium that held more than 700 people. We would be able to grow significantly while we continued our search for a plot of land on which to build our church home. The elder board prayed about it and agreed it was God's purpose for us to move so we contacted the local school board to see whether we could enter a lease agreement with them to use their building on Sundays. The school board's response surprised us. They offered us a one-month lease, and if things worked well, they would renew the lease on a month-to-month basis indefinitely. We were in a building where we could have stayed as long as we wanted, although if we did, we would have found it necessary to change our mission, because we would not have been able to reach more and more people with the new life of Jesus. Moving to the school would give us the opportunity to reach a virtually unlimited number of people with the new life of Jesus, but with the possibility of being out on the street every thirty days. We decided to step out in faith once again and move to the school. We prepared to make the move in April of 2003, although the term *we* wasn't exactly what I expected.

The Big Mistake

During the process of getting ready to move from Ivywood to the school, we held several meetings to cast the vision of why it was necessary for us to move. As always the focus was on reaching more people in Jesus' name, and sharing the new life of Jesus with the world, starting in our own communities. During one of those meetings I made a big mistake, perhaps the biggest mistake I have ever made from a strategic standpoint when it comes to moving our mission forward. There might be no one, who is part of New Life today who remembers it, but I remember it as if it were yesterday. I was talking about the challenges of worshiping at the school, and of being in a place we could use only on Sundays. We would have to set up all of the sound equipment every week, all of the hospitality tables and equipment, all of the children's ministry equipment. Then when we were done, we would have to store it in a trailer and do it all again the next week. I told everyone each of us would need to be part of that because lost people are worth it.

That's when I made the mistake. I said, "Even if I have to set up everything myself every week, we are going to make this move." My intention was to make it clear this move was so vital to our mission that we *were* going to make it. If I had to see to it personally that it happened, I would. That was a major mistake on two levels. First, God was the one who would make the move work, or not work. We were making the move because we had discerned it was His will for us, not because I was going to make sure we continued to reach lost people. Second, I was saying everyone else's help was optional. The truth was we were about to need each other more than we ever had in New Life's brief history. So far everything had been easy. So far everything had been amazing. God was being praised. People were being saved. Ministries were growing and nearly everyone was positive about the future. All of that was about to change in a heartbeat.

I had overestimated the people's level of buy-in for our mission of sharing the new life of Jesus Christ with the world — one person at a time. I anticipated losing some people in the transition from Ivywood to the school, perhaps as many as thirty. I knew it would be hard for some to leave a "church" building to worship in a school, and for others to care more about people who weren't even part of New Life or God's Kingdom yet, than for their own needs. When we made the move to the school, our weekend worship attendance dropped from more than two hundred and twenty people to about a hundred and seventy. Then it continued dropping over the next year until it reached a low of about a hundred and fifty. We had lost more than twice the number of folks I had anticipated.

Many folks remained committed to the mission of sharing Jesus' new life with others, but during that time it became hard not to wonder where everybody had gone. As we looked around the massive auditorium and saw a hundred and fifty people scattered about, it seemed like "no one" was there. I probably prayed more during that period of New Life's young history than I had at any time in my life up to that point. It would have been a good time for God to speak audibly.

He didn't.

Always Darkest

The next several years challenged the very existence of New Life. While most new churches in America fail in the first five years, New Life had started out well and seemed to be sailing through the first five years. We were in year three when it became extremely difficult. I don't know whether you have ever gone through a time when you questioned whether you had done the right thing, not in a casual way, but in earnest because you had invested everything. That's what it was like during those next several years. It seemed people often questioned whether we had made the right decision in moving to the school. The building was too big, too cold, too dark, and despite being called an auditorium the sound wasn't very good. The children's ministry area wasn't ideal. (The nursery was the school's detention room during the week.) Set up and tear down wasn't much fun, and often relied on a handful of folks. When I had said if I had to do everything myself, it never came to that, but a small group of extremely dedicated folks carried most of the weight for setting up and tearing down week after week.

It's easy to rally around the flag when you're experiencing victory after victory, as we had in the first two years of our life together. But we didn't see many victories during the next several years. I had never pastored a church in numerical decline. Without a building during the week where we could do ministry, we had to be creative. For a while we did youth ministry at various members' homes. Eventually, we rented a building from another local church, which made things somewhat better, but the overall attitude during those few years was less than optimistic. We needed something to show us God was still with us, as He had been so clearly when we launched New Life.

Land, Ho!

As we weathered the doldrums that seemed to be more and more pervasive, God finally opened a door—literally. We had continued to look for a plot of land. In December 2004, someone told one of our elders that a twenty-acre plot of land was going to become available soon on Knoch Road. It was only a mile and a half from the school, and in a much more visible and accessible location than Ivywood. He suggested we contact the owner before he put it on the market. On December 19, 2004, elder Frank Relihan and I prayer walked the land. It was a bitterly cold morning with a wind chill factor of twelve degrees so we didn't stay long. As we were leaving, I took a business card from my wallet, and wrote a brief note on it that said,

"If you would like to invest in the Kingdom of God, please give us a call." I stuck the note in the storm door and we got in the car to leave.

Frank asked me, "Why didn't you leave the card in the mailbox?"

"I don't know," I said. "Something told me to leave it in the door." I would soon find it wasn't something, but Someone. I drove past the property on a regular basis for the next couple of weeks, but each time the card was still in the door. We decided to call for a day of prayer and fasting on the first Tuesday in January to ask God for His favor with finding property. That afternoon, my phone rang. The man on the other end told me he was the nephew of the man who owned the property on Knoch Road. He asked whether I would like to get together to talk about purchasing it. We set up the time, and right before the man hung up, he asked, "By the way, why did you leave your business card in the storm door, instead of the mailbox?"

"I don't know. Something told me to leave it in the door," I said.

"It's a good thing you did," he replied. "I never check the mail box, because I have all of Uncle George's mail forwarded to our house." One more coincidence; one more time God spoke to us without saying a word, and it couldn't have come at a better time.

The process of purchasing the land gave us a boost as a church family, and helped move us forward in our life together, but the next few years seemed to be a period of taking a few steps forward and then a couple of steps back. At one point, the school moved us out of the auditorium in order to perform major renovations. During that time they gave us the cafeteria of the primary school, which was located across the street. That move proved to be a major improvement. It was still available only on Sundays and, eventually, Saturday evenings, but it was much newer, brighter, and smaller.

Attendance turned around a bit while we worshiped there. The smaller, more intimate surroundings seemed to fit our now smaller church family. Then the school district moved us back across the street when the auditorium was completed. Many of the same struggles we had faced before returned. It didn't take long before we noticed attendance was starting to decline. Pastor Brad French, our worship and youth pastor suggested we return to the primary school. The elder board prayed about it and discussed it. We finally agreed to move back to the primary school, but this time we would stay there until we were able to construct our first building at the church property.

During that time, the hope of building our own mission outpost on the church property was a vision that sometimes seemed like a hallucination. We formed a team to start planning the construction of our first building. (I say first building, because we sensed from the time we purchased the land that New Life would continue to reach lost people and grow to the point we would outgrow the first building.) The team met for months and months but wasn't able to develop a viable proposal for our first building. We knew God had given us the land to use for advancing His Kingdom, but we couldn't seem to discern exactly what that would look like, or how we would be able to pay for it.

A Strategy at Last

As we prayed and struggled with many questions about the land, the building, and the future of New Life, we heard about a group called Harvestime. The group's purpose was to help local churches develop master plans and strategies for accomplishing their missions. It was 2008. We had been at the school for five years, had owned the land for three, and while we had started to see a small but consistent increase in the number of folks being saved, baptized and joining us for worship, the challenges of the weekly set up and tear down were starting to take their toll. The elder board decided to make a substantial financial commitment to partner with Harvestime. As part of the process, the staff would travel to Colorado for a weeklong consultation with them. That would prove to be one of the most God-directed decisions the board ever made.

As we were flying to Colorado, I got out a legal pad and had one of my straightforward conversations with God. I knew a lot of the larger churches around the country had laid out their "strategy" in concise statements based on acrostics of their names, so I said, "God, we need a 'NEWLIFE' strategy." As I wrote each letter of NEWLIFE down the left side of the page, and started to pray and reflect on what each letter might mean, I paused to listen, as in listen for what God would say. No audible response came, but I received promptings as I reflected on each letter. "W" stood for winning the lost. "I" stood for indigenous worship. By the time most of the letters were used up, I realized I was missing a couple of major areas of emphasis—small groups and ministry with children and youth. I added XN to the end of the acrostic since the church's website is www.newlifexn.org. The "X" stood for eXtensive small group ministry, and the second "N" stood for Next generation focus. A couple of the letters weren't exactly right, but it was a good start.

During our time with Harvestime, we filled in the blanks in what we came to call the !NEWLIFEXN! Mission Strategy. Pat Fecich, our pastor of administration, added the exclamation points at the beginning and end of the acrostic. They stand for prayer, because at New

Life everything begins and ends with prayer. It made a powerful addition to the strategy. Eventually, the entire acrostic stood for: !-Prayer; N-Noticing and Welcoming Guests; E-Equipping Leaders; W-Winning the Lost; L-Life Management; I-Indigenous Worship; F-Focus on Men; E-Everyone in Ministry; X-eXtensive Small Group Ministry; N-Next Generation Focus; and !-Prayer. This brief strategy has helped us discern whether a ministry or direction fits in our overall mission of New Life many times in the years since we hammered it out together back in 2008.

During that week, Harvestime also helped us picture a master plan for the church property. It included a three-phase process that would allow us to start with something functional and affordable, and move to our maximum capacity of serving 1,600 to 2,000 people per weekend. This was a major step of faith considering we are located in a rural area, and at the time our average Sunday worship attendance was about 170 people. While we have revised the master plan many times since that week, it gave us a tangible and realistic starting point from which we were able to move forward.

Many people have been credited with the quote, "Failing to plan is planning to fail." At New Life, Pat had always reminded us of that truth, but it was through our week together as a staff in 2008 that God brought us a plan and strategy for making our mission become more and more a reality. In fact, while we saw only marginal steps toward accomplishing our mission in the years 2003-2008, from 2008 forward we have seen God accomplish more than we could have ever imagined. God has used many different ordinary individuals to bring those strategies and plans to reality. He used a small team of New Life staff that week in 2008 to bring clarity to our work together that had never been recognized or put into action to that point.

Information – Application = Information, but...

In the summer of 2009, Emmy petitioned Nancy and me to invest three weeks instead of her usual one week at the orphanage construction project in Mexico. We had been working there each summer since that first fall trip back in 2001. While Emmy was now fifteen, three weeks seemed like a long time to us. One of the weeks was to be New Life's annual trip week, but for the other two Emmy would serve as staff for the orphanage project. Nancy and I were in favor of Emmy's pursuit of her dream to one day serve as a missionary pediatrician at the orphanage, and her pursuit of God's work in her life in general, but it was challenging to think of the three-week commitment in an area that wasn't completely "safe." (I put "safe" in quotes because we all know no place is completely safe in this world.) As we prayed and considered Emmy's request, we came to the conclusion I would take two weeks of study leave and stay at the orphanage while Emmy worked there. I would also participate in New Life's annual trip, which I always did anyway. Emmy could pursue her passion for mission, and Nancy and I would be comforted in knowing I was there.

One afternoon during our time there, I started focusing on New Life's small group ministry. I was thinking about why it seemed that small groups, adult classes, and even weekend messages seemed to produce so little change in people's everyday lives. As I thought about it two formulas came to my mind: Information – Application = Information; and Information + Application = Transformation. That was it! I realized instantly that all too often folks wanted another class on evangelism, for example, but then didn't apply the information they had learned in their daily experiences with folks who don't know Jesus. One more class, or one more small group, or one more message where we take notes and then file them away somewhere doesn't change anyone.

The concept is so simple, but not easy to apply. After all, accumulating information is safe and easy. It requires no risk, and only a small amount of work. On the other hand, applying the information we gain from the Bible can be quite risky — a person could end up serving in a foreign country, in a place that isn't safe, for weeks, months, or even a lifetime. This breakthrough led to a change in the way I prepared messages, and how I led small groups and other classes. As I prepared, I asked myself, "What do I want the participant to *apply* from taking part in this opportunity?"

It may seem obvious to you that Information – Application = Information and that Information + Application = Transformation, but those two formulas have helped us to see the end goal of everything we do at New Life is to have our lives transformed, to become more and more like Jesus. I hope as you have been reading this book you have come across at least one piece of information that you have committed to apply in your own life so Jesus can transform you from the inside out. If even one person who has read to this point has the same *Aha!* moment that I had when those two formulas came to me, and starts adding the "+" between information and application, it will be more than worth the time we've invested in writing and reading it.

Send Us Men

You might have noticed when you read the !NEWLIFEXN! strategy the "F" stands for Focus on Men, but there's no focus on women. You might have wondered: *Why a focus on men, but not on women?* The answer is simple; in my experience women have a much more natural inclination to pursue God's transforming presence in their lives than men. Women have a much more natural tendency to seek out supportive relationships than men. While the world has changed dramatically in my lifetime, one of the realities that has remained true statistically is many more women than men participate in the worship and ministries of local churches. When I was a boy growing up in Gipsy, men were noticeably absent from Gipsy Christian Church. Women far outnumbered men. Statistically, six out of ten participants in churches across America are women. When we started New Life, I determined to do all I could to attract men to the church. I started with prayer. I prayed to God regularly, "Send us men."

Since becoming a pastor, I have always sought to live in a way that normal men would see as normal too. I didn't want to be one more religious leader who doesn't have any clue about the real challenges of real men. I've always remembered Dr. Willis's challenge not to let my three years (which became six years when I pursued my doctor of ministry degree) of theological education turn me into a poor marksman when it came to sharing and living the truth of God in Jesus Christ. My experience as a carpenter has given me the opportunity to relate to blue-collar workers over the years in ways that the typical academic type may not be able to do. New Life's focus on men was a natural outgrowth of my desire to see men represented equally in the church, because nearly 50 percent of the general population is men.

In the spring of 2010, God answered my prayer to send us men in a way I never anticipated. A halfway house for men in recovery from alcoholism and other drug addictions had opened near us in

January. One of their workers asked a friend of hers who served on our worship team if it would be okay for a couple of the guys to come to worship on Easter. She wasn't sure whether they would be welcomed. We assured her everyone is welcome at New Life, so a couple of guys from the house joined us for worship. The next week four guys from the house worshiped with us.

In the weeks that followed the numbers increased. That summer one of the guys asked me if I would consider leading a weekly Bible study at the house, which I did. That Bible study continues to the present and now fifteen to twenty guys from the house worship with us most weekends. It's funny how God will answer our prayers in ways we never would have imagined, and what He will do through us when we apply His information to our lives in those moments. Hundreds of men have been part of New Life during their stays at the halfway house. Many of them have come to know Jesus as their Savior and Lord and been baptized through that experience. I thank God that He continues to answer my prayer to send us men every single week so we can share the truth and love of Jesus with them, and they can experience His transformation through us.

I have also led men's small groups and men's classes at New Life. I want the men to know they are important to God and that they have a vital role to play in our life together. I have always had an accountability partner during my time at Glade Run and New Life. In addition to Nancy, who is my first and closest accountability partner, Bill Gebhart has been my accountability partner for more than twenty years. In that one-on-one relationship, Bill and I have helped each other to be more faithful men of God, husbands, and dads. We have used the Bible to guide us in our day-to-day work and relationships too.

This focus on men that starts with my accountability partner extends through leading groups of men in the New Life family, welcomes men from the halfway house, and moves ultimately through all of our relationships in the community is a vital part of New Life's ministry, and of my life as a man. When I think of sharing, growing and living the new life of Jesus Christ with the world — one person at a time — I often remember each of us is unique, and while God addresses all of us as His children through Jesus, He also relates to each of us in our uniqueness. Being a man is part of my uniqueness, and I'm grateful for the opportunity to help other men see what that means in their unique relationships with God through Jesus Christ.

The Tragedy That Brought Triumph

On November 1, 2011, Nancy and I went to bed a little before ten o'clock. My cell phone rang shortly after that, and although I was drifting off to sleep it woke me. I went to the kitchen where I keep the phone at night and answered it. I will always remember the words I heard, "Pastor Chris. This is Tammy Summers. Our daughter, Alex, has been in a car accident and the police have told us she did not survive." For a moment, I didn't respond. I was hoping I hadn't heard what I knew I had. The final phrase seemed to echo, "…she did not survive." I got the details about the location of the accident and told Tammy I would be there as soon as I could.

The accident site was only about ten minutes from our home so I got there quickly. As I started to turn onto the road, I saw it was closed and an EMS worker was standing there holding a flare. I told him I was the pastor of the girl in the accident and that her parents had called and asked me to come. He radioed his supervisor and I was told to park my car. One of the EMS people drove me down to the site. I got out and walked past Alex's car to Brian and Tammy who were standing outside of their car on the other side of the accident. When I got to them, I hugged them, and then we got into the car. We talked briefly about what had happened, the details of which were uncertain at the moment. Then Tammy said, "Pastor Chris, you have to preach a gospel message at Alex's funeral." I was amazed. Brian and Tammy had lost a young son to a childhood illness years before, and now their beautiful, teenage daughter was dead, too. In the midst of that Tammy's concern was the people who came to Alex's funeral would hear the good news of Jesus' salvation.

Brian and Tammy asked me if I would go over to the car and say a prayer. They had not been permitted to go to the car, and they wanted someone to be there. They knew Alex was dead, but they wanted me to offer a prayer of thanksgiving for her life. The police and emergency workers gave me permission. When I walked over to the car, it was one of the most difficult moments of my life. Not only was I grieving for Brian and Tammy's loss, for the loss of Alex who was coming into the prime of her life, but also, the color of Alex's hair was nearly the same as Emmy's. As I looked at Alex, I pictured Emmy. It made me realize how fragile each of our lives is, and how important it is for us to know Jesus as Savior and Lord. Brian and Tammy's strength through that moment and through the years since the accident have been one of the clearest testimonies I've experienced of the power of faith in Jesus Christ.

I spent most of that night with the Summers family. We prayed together in their car at the accident site. Then I went to their home. Many of their relatives came, along with some of Alex's friends, and a few other folks from New Life. What I will always remember from that night is how Brian, and especially Tammy, comforted those who came to comfort them. Only later would Brian tell me that it was that night that he got down on his knees and committed his life to Jesus fully. In the years since that moment Brian has joined Tammy in sharing their faith with hundreds of people both one-on-one and in groups. The power of their faith is tangible, and God has used it to open doors to many people.

Neither Brian nor Tammy would ever have wished to lose Alex, but, I have heard both of them say, "We didn't lose Alex. We know exactly where she is, and we will see her again in Heaven." Those are not shallow or empty words coming from Brian and Tammy. They believe them with all of their hearts, and they have become stronger and stronger as time has passed — that is one of the many triumphs to come from Alex's tragedy.

November 1 was a Tuesday. Throughout the week, the small town of Saxonburg where we live came together as I have never seen happen during such a tragic event. More than a thousand people went to the visitation at the funeral home in nearby Butler, and Saxonburg Memorial Presbyterian Church offered us the use of their worship center for Alex's funeral, because we still didn't have a building at the time. The funeral itself was one of the most incredible experiences I have ever had the opportunity to share. When I gave folks the opportunity to come forward to offer a remembrance of what Alex had meant in their lives, more than seventy people came forward. Most of them were students, and their experiences ranged from being a cheerleader with Alex to being someone who missed the bus, and Alex waited with him until his father came to take him home. Alex's life was truly a light to those around her. Ten people trusted Jesus as Savior and Lord at that funeral service.

Much more could be said about the impact of Alex's death and how God used it for triumph that week and in the time since, but the Sunday after Alex died, I changed my message to address how God works in community during times of pain and loss. Our weekly worship attendance had grown to about 250 people per weekend by that time, but 350 people worshiped with us that weekend.

We were soon to find this was not a one-time event where people gathered because of their great loss, only to go back to life as normal the next week. That's what happened after 9/11 in 2001. Churches across America doubled and tripled in attendance the Sunday after that tragic event, but within a few weeks it was back to business as usual. The same thing happened at New Life. The weekend after 9/11, more than 300 people worshiped with us, but the extra folks didn't come back the next week. The week after the 350 people showed up to experience God's comfort and guidance following Alex's death, 350 people came again. It was the same the next week. We closed out 2011 with an average worship attendance of more than 260 people per week for the year and 2012 with an average worship attendance of 375 people per week. Much of that growth was directly attributable to God taking a terrible tragedy and turning it into triumph in people's lives, and particularly in Brian and Tammy's lives. As they continued to praise God in the midst of their personal loss, many came to hear God's voice through theirs.

Please, understand that Alex's death at such a young age was and is a tragedy. But God has used it for so much good. The Apostle Paul reminded us in Romans 8:28, "And we know God causes everything to work together for the good of those who love God and are called according to his purpose for them." We have seen this in so many tangible ways: It drew the school and community closer together; people came to understand their meaning and purpose in life through coming to trust Jesus as their Savior and Lord; a scholarship fund was established in Alex's memory that has helped young people attend college; our daughter Emmy wrote a beautiful tribute song that was sung by the school choir at their graduation; and much more.

All of that does not make Alex's death less tragic. It makes the reality of God's goodness that much more vital, because sin and death will always take their toll in our world, and we must turn to God to bring meaning and purpose to us when we experience their impact. He doesn't make the bad things good. He brings good in the midst of them. William P. Young wrote in *The Shack*, "Grace does not depend on suffering to exist, but where there is suffering, you will find grace in many facets and colors."

It Doesn't Matter What You Believe

As you read the account of Alex's death and what God has done in the aftermath, you might have thought, "But couldn't God have kept her from dying in the first place?" Or similarly, "That's why I don't believe in God. How could a good God allow a teenager with so much going for her die?" We live in a culture that has many views of God and an increasing number of folks who don't believe in God at all. We've been told on the one hand that we need to be tolerant of everyone's views of God because all religions teach the same, basic truths in the end. Or, on the other hand, people say we'd all be better off if religion were eliminated because it causes so much conflict in the world.

As I've said, it's beyond the scope of this book to address such matters in depth, but I do want to add one point that Emmy showed me in a book titled *One Thing You Can't Do in Heaven*. The author made this statement: "It doesn't matter what you believe. It matters what's true." Look at that statement again: "It doesn't matter what you believe. It matters what's true." I believe Jesus Christ is the Son of the living God. I believe God created the universe and all it contains. I believe God lives in each of us who know Jesus Christ as Savior and Lord through the Holy Spirit.

At the end of the day, it doesn't matter what I believe. It matters what's true. When people say all religions have the same basic goals and beliefs, I know that isn't true. I've had the opportunity to talk with many Hindus and Buddhists about their views of the afterlife. Because they both believe in reincarnation of the dead to another life as a human being or other creature, and I believe people die once and spend eternity in either Heaven or Hell, I have asked them, "Would you agree when it comes to the afterlife, either you are right and I am wrong, or I am right and you are wrong, or we are both wrong, but we both can't be right?" After they have understood my statement every, single Hindu or Buddhist I have ever asked this question has agreed with me. All religions teach radically different "truths," and therefore they can't all be right.

I was once speaking with a man at the halfway house who told me he was an atheist. He had been sleeping in the room where we were going to hold the Bible study, and when one of the other guys woke him and told him what was going on, he said, "I'm outta here." When I found out he was leaving because he was an atheist, I asked him why he was an atheist? He said, "Only a fool would believe there's a god."

I said, "That's funny."

"What do you mean?" he asked.

"The Bible says only a fool would believe there is no God," I replied. He and I bantered back and forth good-naturedly for a while and then he said,

"Look, here's the bottom line: You think I'm going to Hell when I die because I don't believe in Jesus, right?"

I said, "The Bible teaches if you don't believe in Jesus you will go to Hell when you die, so yes, I believe that."

"Well, I don't believe in Hell," he countered.

"If I were to knock you out right now and put you in the trunk of my car and drive you to Texas; when you woke up, if you didn't believe in Texas, where would you be?" I asked.

He knew I had him, but he countered, "Well, if I didn't believe in Texas, I wouldn't think I was in Texas."

"But where would you be?" I asked again.

"Texas, I guess," he said.

I said, "It doesn't matter what you believe. It matters what's true." I went on to acknowledge I can't "prove" we go to Heaven or Hell when we die, but the evidence for Jesus being whom He said He was is strong, as is the evidence for a creator of the universe rather than the popular view that everything happened by random chance. The man stayed for the rest of the study, and eventually came to believe in God. The point isn't that everyone who gives serious thought to what they believe will come to recognize the truth of Jesus' claims. The point is, while many in our day claim there is no absolute truth, or that all truth claims are equally valid, those are beliefs not truths, and it doesn't matter what you believe. It matters what's true. I hope you are one who holds onto truth, or has at least examined the truth claims of atheism, Buddhism, Islam, Christianity and other belief systems to see how they measure up to the standard of truth. In the end it does matter what's true.

Half Measures

One of the blessings of investing an hour every week with the guys at the halfway house Bible study over the past six years is I have picked up some of the language of Alcoholics Anonymous (AA). My favorite quote is: "Half measures have availed me nothing." Many times over the years, I've found myself resorting to "half measures." I haven't given my full effort to a task, belief, or relationship.

The result of half measures is nothing. This book is a perfect example. It started out as a book for men, based on New Life's focus on men. I thought it would take me a few days to write. Then, based on prayer time with God, the focus of the book changed to *Life Planning*. As I sat down to write that book, I realized as great as the book might be, I wasn't even giving the process half measures in my own life. How could such a book help others? Then I changed the focus to *A Funny Thing Happened**. I started writing and the book flowed, because it was a topic that fully engaged my heart and mind. Even so, I didn't take the time to sit down regularly to write. The truth is I wrote most of this book over a two-day period, when I was fully invested in writing. I gave it everything I had—no more half measures. I never cease to amaze myself with how often I default to half measures. Whether it's in something simple like daily exercise, or something dramatic like writing a book, when I give everything I have something good happens. When I give everything I have and call on the Holy Spirit to do more than I can do, He always does, and great things happen.

I know this is true, but as Leo Buscaglia said decades ago, "To know and not to do is not yet to know."

You might be a person who is always "all in." You might not be a half-measure kind of person, but, if you are, I want to challenge and encourage you to choose something simple and go all in for a change. The world is filled with half-measure people, who hope to do something big someday, or even something small. The only way that's ever going to happen is to give it everything. My guess is you have a book in you, or a home project, or a different vocation, or a healthier life, or _____ (you fill in the blank). All it needs to come out is a commitment to stay with it, and the Holy Spirit's encouragement and power. It is not coincidental that the statement: Half measures have availed me nothing, comes from a recovery group. Anyone who has ever attempted to overcome an addiction knows you can't recover halfway. (Haven't all of us had some kind of addiction or addictive process going on in our lives that we needed to overcome?)

When Everything Is Going Right and Nothing Is

As I write these words nearly everything is going right at New Life at the moment. Our staff has grown from that small, handful of folks who went to Colorado in 2008 to nearly twenty full-time and part-time staff. Our weekend worship attendance is approaching 800, and we're getting ready to add the second phase building from our master plan. While it's always dangerous to measure success by a growing number of people attending a church, as Dr. Samuel

Moffett said in a Missions class at Princeton Seminary, "While the presence of numbers of people is not always a sign of growth in a local church, it's usually a better indicator than an absence of them." After all, we're not talking about numbers; we're talking about people. People are committing their lives to Jesus on a weekly basis. Folks are being baptized. The youth ministry is growing. Children are experiencing the truth and love of Jesus and we are planning a Children's Nurture and Discipleship Center where they'll have an even better place to learn and grow. More folks are using their gifts and talents in ministry in, through and beyond New Life than ever before. There's a general sense of wellbeing among the folks of New Life. From that standpoint everything is going right.

At the same time, Abby and Emmy are not following Jesus right now. Each of our daughters grew up being integrally involved in the life of New Life and much more importantly in pursuing their own faith. As with many of us, they are challenging the beliefs of their childhoods. Each of us must do that at some point, or risk living our entire lives through someone else's faith. Having said that, as a parent who loves his daughters more than life itself, it feels as if nothing is going right when they aren't "on the bus," at the moment. I believe they will return to putting Jesus first in their lives, and often remember Jesus' words to Peter, on the night before He was crucified. Jesus told Peter he would deny Jesus three times that night. Peter had protested loudly he would go to prison and death before he ever denied Jesus. Jesus closed His comments to Peter by saying, "When you return, strengthen your brothers." When you return. Not if you return, but *when* you return. Peter did deny Jesus and he did return to Him.

I know many of you reading this book find yourself in the same situation. You have been faithful to God, as have your children. Then one day your child tells you he or she doesn't believe what you believe. In that moment nothing is right, especially if your faith is central to your life, if you are all in with your faith. As I have prayed, reflected, cried and called out to God for His help in bringing the girls back to Him, I have been reminded God is not in the practice of forcing us to do anything. I have taken many missteps along the way, and have blatantly sinned many times.

My crisis of faith was short-lived. Shortly after I had my powerful experience of the Holy Spirit's presence in my life, I decided I was going to give up on God. After all, the constant tension of my goal of becoming rich and famous bumping up against His plan of me serving as a pastor was often overwhelming. I decided I would stop believing in Jesus. I purposed to become like Spock on Star Trek. Although I couldn't be a Vulcan, I could live my life calmly, coolly, and logically. I would be in charge.

Only I couldn't do it.

My experiment lasted for about two weeks. I would say, "I don't believe in God," and even as I said it, my heart would be saying: *Yes, you do!* I have always had an academic bent. I love reading, learning, and pursuing knowledge. At the same time, God has always given me the gift of faith. I have examined the evidence for the existence of God, and specifically for the existence of a theistic God, and found it logically compelling. I have examined further and found of the three major theistic frames of reference: Judaism, Islam and Christianity, Christianity is the most compelling. I don't understand how anyone who examines life seriously can come to another belief. But then faith is my primary gift, so I find it easier to take the small jump from reason to faith than many. Even though I couldn't get the hill behind Gipsy Christian Church to move in Jesus' name when I was a boy; I have seen Him move so many obstacles in my life since then that I can do nothing other than believe.

I share this because at the end of the day we are all called to live our lives in relationship and community with others. We all tend toward isolation. That has been our bent since sin entered the world. We Americans live in a culture that is increasingly individualistic. We often think our individual frame of reference is *the* frame of reference. We pick and choose what to think, believe, and live as if life is a smorgasbord that exists to satisfy us. Even my statement that everything is right, while nothing is right buys into our culture's understanding that the rightness and wrongness of life has to do with my personal satisfaction or yours.

The truth is only God has the right to determine what is good, true, loving and right. He did so long ago. Because of sin's entrance into the world shortly after creation, we human beings will always be swimming upstream when we seek to follow God's goodness, truth, love and righteousness. Thankfully, He came in the man, Jesus Christ, to show us what that looks like in human form. He has also promised to be with us *always* as we engage the process. Throughout my life, I have experienced the truth of that promise as God has spoken to me through His word, through prayer, through circumstances and through other people. I haven't always listened well, and surely haven't always done what I knew to be true. Even so, God continues to speak, and to be true to Himself. He cannot do otherwise. That means whether all is going right or whether nothing is from our perspective, we are, as the Apostle Paul put it nearly

2000 years ago, "...more than conquerors through Christ Jesus who loves us!"

The Next Right Thing

My second favorite AA saying is, "Do the next right thing." I like the saying so much because it reminds us how simple following Jesus is. It's not easy to follow Jesus, but it is simple. All we have to do at any given moment is the next right thing. How will we know what the next right thing is? We learn it in God's word. We call out to Him and ask. We let the Holy Spirit work in and through us. We rejoice in the moments when we are certain God has told or shown us what to do. We hold on to Him tightly when we don't know what the next right thing is, and we don't let go until He shows us.

When we fail?

We repent. We turn back to God and we start again. So many times in my life, taking a wrong turn has paralyzed me. I have not been paralyzed because I have taken the wrong turn, but because I have been too stubborn to turn back. That has been literally true when I've been driving (before the days of GPS), and spiritually true on so many more occasions. I am so grateful God loves me—period; not because I am good—I learned I am not good when I was five; not because I have stopped doing bad—I still take wrong turns far too often; but because I am His child.

When I became the dad of two daughters who decided to walk the wrong path for a time, I discovered more than ever before something of what it must feel like to be God. He has nearly seven billion children, and not one of us walks the right path all the time. Yet, He keeps offering us truth, love, grace, and forgiveness. Those are always the next right things. When we find ourselves not knowing what the next right thing is, we'll never go wrong by choosing truth, love, grace and forgiveness.

Ordinary People

If I asked you, "Do you want to be an ordinary person?" You would almost certainly say, "No." We are a people of superlatives. We sell totally awesome cleaners. We buy incredible washers and dryers. We drive sexy cars and trucks. We would never want ordinary to be the descriptor for our lives or for us, yet it is. When compared to the God who created us we are ordinary. The prophet Isaiah told us as high as the heavens are above the earth, so are God's thoughts higher than our thoughts and his ways higher than our ways. Wow. That's incredibly higher. Yet, King David reminded us God made us a little lower than Himself. God sees us as extraordinary beings because He sees us through a parent's eyes, a perfect parent's eyes. When we are tempted to fall into the world's illusion that we are awesome, incredible or extraordinary based on what we accomplish, or how much we have, or how we look, or how much we know, or where we rank on the company's org chart, we must always remember—God has our picture on His refrigerator.

That is our only claim to being extraordinary. You know what I mean, right? All loving moms and dads have pictures of their children on their refrigerators at some point. Maybe it's cut out of the local newspaper and commemorates a sporting accomplishment, or participation in the school play. Maybe it's the most recent school picture, or a picture with a cousin, uncle, or grandma. The pictures are there simply to remind us that our children are *our* children, and for that reason alone, they are extraordinary to us.

I know every child hasn't experienced that. Not every mom or dad takes the time to put a picture on the refrigerator, and some children don't have moms or dads. Such children can think of themselves as ordinary or even worthless. That's the problem with viewing matters from a worldly perspective. We tend to exaggerate the good as well as the bad, because only through comparison do we feel special, different or more than ordinary.

It took me a long time to realize being rich and famous wouldn't make me extraordinary, or even memorable. Far too many of us pursue paths we think will bring us a sense of meaning and purpose because some teacher, guidance counselor, or even parent told us it would be the only way to set ourselves apart from the rest. The truth is long before we were born, or as my mother used to say, "Long before you were a gleam in your father's eye," God had an extraordinary plan for you and me. Only as we live out that plan will we know the joy of living extraordinary lives.

Extraordinary God

Yes, God is extraordinary. In so many ways God goes beyond what we could ever expect Him to be or do. For me the most extraordinary truth about God is while He created the universe and all it contains, while He has infinite cosmic power, He cares for you and me—and every person on the earth—as if we were the only person on the earth. How can God keep us all sorted out? Why would He want to? What value does He see in us when we so easily and so often turn away from Him, and by our words or actions tell Him He doesn't exist?

The God of the Bible is extraordinary. As Karl Barth said, "God is not man shouted in a loud voice." We may not believe in Him, but He believes in us. He continues to reach into our lives, to offer us the life that is truly life, through Jesus. My hope and prayer is you have seen glimpses of Him as you have read these pages; that you have heard Him speak to you, as I have heard Him speak to me throughout my life.

The Solution

If you have never experienced this extraordinary God, the solution is simple. Not easy, but simple: Trust His Son, Jesus as your Lord. That means Jesus becomes the owner of your life. Trust Him as your Savior. That means He saves you from sin and death and for a life of truth and love now and forever.

Many have said it's too simple. There has to be more to it than that. Oh, there is. There is so much more than trusting Jesus as Savior and Lord. In that instant the ownership of your life transfers from you to Him. From that moment forward you belong to Him. He promises never to leave you nor forsake you. He gives you His Holy Spirit to empower you to obey His commands, and to be transformed from the inside out. The good news is after that you won't become better by working harder. In fact, you *can't* become better by working harder. We aren't saved by God's grace and then transformed by our efforts. We are saved and transformed by the very same grace. Day-by-day, as you surrender your will to His, you will receive fresh mercy and grace for each new day. It is the life that is truly life, and when compared with anything the world has to offer it is truly extraordinary.

If you have already experienced the new life Jesus offers, but the joy has waned, the extraordinary has become ordinary; if everything is right, but nothing is, I know the feeling. We all do at some point. In those moments, remember He never changes. He is the same yesterday, today, and forever. That means His joy and power are available now as it was yesterday, or ten years ago. That means the extraordinary plan God has for us is still in front of you and me.

Some days will feel mundane because some days all we can do is persevere. Some days will feel incredible because some days God sets amazing opportunities and blessings in front of us. Some days will feel scary because our enemy the devil does not want us to experience the extraordinary life God created us to live. Some days will seem hopeless because we don't see what God sees as we take the next step. Some days we will tell God He doesn't exist and we're not going to follow Him anymore. The funny thing is it doesn't matter how we feel about God or what we tell Him. In all of those moments, and days, and many more, our extraordinary God is for us and with us — He simply wants to be *with* us…

How extraordinary is that?

About the Author

C hris Marshall is an ordinary person who serves the extraordinary God of the universe as the Lead Pastor of New Life Christian Ministries in Saxonburg, PA. New Life is a non-denominational church that he and Nancy, his wife, planted in April of 2001 to share the new life of Jesus Christ with the world — one person at a time! In July of 2016 as New Life celebrated her fifteenth anniversary the mission was expanded: To share, grow and live the new life of Jesus Christ with the world — one person at a time, because as we mature in the Lord we move beyond sharing the new life to growing and living it, too.

Chris has also written *Life Cycle of a Christian: A User's Guide to Life After Rebirth,* and *An Amazing Tale: And Other Stories of Jesus' Birth.*

Chris welcomes your comments about *A Funny Thing Happened on the Way to the Beach.** Chris writes regularly at ChrisMarshallResources. com. His blog is titled *Helping Leaders Lead Better.* You can reach him via Chris@ChrisMarshallResources.com.